I have taught leadership programs for the last 40 plus years and I have studied principles written by some of the best authors in the world. I became a collector of many ideas and thoughts from these authors and even included how to win a war using the Principles of War from our United States Military. Coupled with my own experiences of managing a multibillion dollar bank holding company, I became invited all over the country to speak. Now retired and wishing that I would have had the writings and thoughts from Matt Kutz, how much better I would have been. His book is state of the art and should be included in discussing any leadership program that is taught today. This is a great book.

Edward J. Reiter
Retired CEO and Chairman
Sky Financial Group (formerly Mid Am Inc.)

Real challenges in organizations are not business challenges like the ability to interpret trends in spreadsheets, tweaking another 2% out of the bottom line, or raising quality scores. The real challenges in organizations are getting people engaged, committed and bridging leaders to adapt during changing circumstances in an unpredictable and constantly changing environment. Matt has the ability to break the bonds that hold you back, unleashing powerful information with his transformative leadership – in sharing his research and application to contextual intelligence. Dr. Kutz is an amazing speaker, writer and thought-leader, and his program on contextual intelligence and 3D thinking – worth the time in reaching your potential.

Debra A. Ball
Vice President, Learning & Service Excellence
ProMedica Health System, Toledo, OH

The tenets of Contextual Intelligence are increasingly critical for today's business leaders. Through both his counsel and presentation, Dr. Kutz skillfully balances academia and real-world, making CI not only relevant for leaders, but actionable.

Patrick Blair, Global Business Services
Procter & Gamble
Cincinnati, OH

If you are ready to go beyond the conventional leadership mantras and gain practical and powerful insights that work in the real world of organizations, this is the book to read. In *3D Thinking*, Dr. Kutz not only introduces the new model of Contextual Intelligence, but unpacks and delivers keen insights on what contextual intelligence behaviors look like. My own experiences in leading people, developing leaders and building organizations were confirmed but also challenged to go higher and deeper with improved hindsight, insight and foresight. If you are an emerging or experienced leader you will not want to miss this book – powerful and compelling!

Bobby Hill, EdD.
Director, Center for Christian Thought and Action
Regent University, Virginia Beach, VA

For some time now I have had an interest in the small c and big C of Context and was delighted to discover the work of Matt about 2 years ago. Matt is a present day leader in this field and his work makes sense and gives meaning to many of the situations we find ourselves in. Today's global uncertainty further increases the relevance and significance of contextual intelligence. The 12 competencies identified by Matt are goal posts for us all to aspire to if we are truly to be leaders of influence. I would recommend Matt's work as a core text for any leadership program.

Dr. Anita Bamford-Wade, D.Nurs. RN
Joint Head of Nursing
Auckland University of Technology, Auckland, NZ

[Dr. Kutz] entices a leader to see beyond strategic planning and look at unique perspectives from their past, present, and future experiences and access them simultaneously into unique leadership behaviors and outcomes. If you are a person that likes to think outside the box, then "Contextual Intelligence" should challenge your preconceived ideas and capture your curiosity about the adaptation to leadership. Dr. Kutz's presentation will put you on the edge and keep you there. I highly recommend this course to anyone that is in management or plans to go there.

    Nelson Evans
    Mayor of Perrysburg, OH

Years of "personality profiles" have emboldened us to stake our claims in the way we think. Too often leaders rely on logic, reason, emotions, and perception to make decisions. Contextual Intelligence goes beyond "the box" – it considers the texture, feel, structure, and environment that "the box" is in. Dr. Kutz has elevated the way we think about thinking.

    Tamar Truett, CLCP
    Director of Volunteer Experiences
    Girl Scouts of Greater Atlanta, Atlanta, GA

Contextual Intelligence is a fresh look at the dynamics of decision making that is both practical and inspired... and is higher learning that actually works in the real world. I have participated in many seminars and leadership trainings, but this is one of the few that actually had people buzzing afterwards. That is because these principles are transformational in your personal life as well as your workplace.

    Jim Oedy, CEO, Community Sports Network;
    Founder YES FM Radio Network
    Toledo, OH

Having attended and managed countless conferences and training sessions [I was skeptical]... I personally attended, brought one of my assistant directors, and invited other colleagues to the event. I was not disappointed. Matt is a dynamic speaker, and he also backs up what he is talking about with research and science. He is introspective and thoughtful, but also engaging and connected to his audience.

Ann M. Light, Assistant Dean
Bowling Green State University
College of Continuing & Extended Education

[Dr. Kutz's] concept of contextual intelligence is truly cutting edge and has the real potential to increase your influence and positively change the way you practice leadership and develop leaders.

Jeffrey Taylor
Senior Vice President of Sales
MEDLAB, Chicago, IL

Dr. Matt Kutz is an inspirational speaker and world renowned scholar for his expertise in contextual intelligence. He is engaging, energetic and authentic and uses his real world experiences in health care and higher education as platforms for illustrating the importance of contextual intelligence in leadership. Dr. Kutz's Contextual Intelligence Inventory™ provides tremendous adaptive insight to organizational leaders, in the midst of change, and serves as a platform for proactively leading the change process. It is hard to imagine anyone who would not benefit from learning more about contextual intelligence!

Gretchen Carroll, Ed.D., J.D., MBA
Director of MBA Program
Tiffin University

My career has spanned several industries and Fortune 500 companies (real estate, telecommunications, public accounting, and education) and taught me this universal truth: most successful leaders and organizations grasp every competitive advantage. With Contextual Intelligence I believe that Dr. Matthew Kutz had discovered a universal advantage; one that every business needs. The ability to teach executives and managers to think like Fortune 500 CEOs and lead like military commanders can take any organization from good to great! Today's uncertain business climate has made forward-looking leadership more difficult and, at the same time, more important. Tomorrow's winners must learn from the past, assess the present and correctly predict the future; all at the same time. That is why the Contextual Intelligence Inventory™ and Dr. Kutz leadership insights are so exciting to me and the administration at the Kings Academy.

Randal Martin, MBA, CPA
Chief Financial Officer, The Kings Academy
Trustee, Palm Beach Atlantic University

The Contextual Intelligence seminar is every bit as exciting and intriguing as the name implies. Learning these concepts is vital for business leaders in these turbulent times. Contextual Intelligence may be just the tool you need to build momentum in the coming years.

Darren T. Munn, CFA
President & Chief Investment Officer
Munn Wealth Management, Maumee, OH

CONTEXTUAL
INTELLIGENCE

ciprofile.com
think 360°. lead your world.

CONTEXTUAL INTELLIGENCE

SMART LEADERSHIP FOR A CONSTANTLY CHANGING WORLD

Matthew R. Kutz, Ph.D.

rtg Publishing
Media Division of Roundtable Group, LLC

Perrysburg, Ohio

While the examples and stories in this book are drawn from real life, the names and any identifying details have been changed or omitted to protect their privacy.

The Contextual Intelligence Model™, the Contextual Intelligence Inventory™ and Contextual Intelligence Profile™ are trademarks of Matthew R Kutz.

ISBN: 978-1-300-21977-4 (paperback)
ISBN: 978-1-304-33778-8 (hardback)
1. Leadership. 2. Organizational management. 3. Business.

Printed in the United States of America
First Edition

To my wife, Angie,

and my sons, Nathan and Jonathan⋯

You ROCK!

TABLE OF CONTENTS

The sons of Issachar who had understanding of the times, to

know what Israel ought to do.

I Chronicles 12:32

Author's Prologue

Today's leadership landscape is far more challenging than it has ever been. Everything is constantly changing. Globalization is becoming universalization. Market drivers constantly reshuffle. Performance indicators are a moving target. Demographics are shifting – sometimes radically. Regulatory policies are always evolving. And global and local contexts continuously recalibrate themselves.

Despite all these factors, businesses are expected to create value in their communities, provide for employees after they retire, solve the world's problems before they think about solving their own, and still be profitable.

As a result, what were once bedrock principles of business leadership are now much less relevant (they might even verge on being *irrelevant*). Traditional theories and assumptions about leadership simply cannot respond to the volatility, uncertainty, complexity, and ambiguity (VUCA) that face organizations operating in a global knowledge economy.

It doesn't matter whether your organization is in the public or the private sector; or whether it's for-profit or non-profit; or whether it's a religious institution or a Fortune 500 company; the VUCA reality of the 21st century landscape will impact how you lead and how you do business.

And yet, the business wisdom that still prevails relies on models, theories, and assumptions that may have been adequate in the not-too-distant past, but show little promise when used today.

For instance, businesses still routinely use performance evaluations that are based on standard job descriptions and simplistic linear thinking, and not the multi-dimensional thinking that is actually needed. Resources are still treated the way they were a century ago. Hiring criteria are still based on scholastic assessment and achievement. Intelligence, data, information, and knowledge – while now viewed as radically different concepts than they once were – are nevertheless measured and treated in the old way.

The education of leaders and the use of leadership models in the 1960's, 1970's, 1980's and early 1990's were based on paradigms rooted in patterns of behavior that were mechanical, predictable, and linear. Work was easily separated from personal life. Office politics were left at the office, and rarely competed with family or personal time. Family, work, religious, and community values were easily separated, as well, and so they rarely conflicted. Market share, too, was easier to calculate and presented fewer variables (a good vision statement could make everything "bad" disappear).

To use a familiar metaphor, the world was flat but turned round overnight. Ironically, the same change-averse phenomenon that occurred during the cognitive transition from a flat world to a round one is happening right now. No one, back then, wanted to risk a long ship journey for fear of falling off the flat world. Similarly, few in the present want to jettison the comfortable business paradigms that have long governed leadership practices.

And yet, many of these perceptual shifts and market changes were first forecast in the 1960's, if not before. So while no one is surprised that leadership has changed so dramatically, the gradual creep of that transition lulled many into a false sense of security. They believed that change would be easy to outrun at any time, and they were busy attending to one more thing that had to come first. Now, however, waking up to the fact that they're out of touch with the present, they either deny it or further entrench themselves in their old behaviors – hoping, perhaps, to will things back to that bygone era in which they were comfortable. Unfortunately, the laws of physics in the 21st century's round world won't allow it.

A new model is needed -- one that is simple to understand and apply, and one that leverages the best of traditional leadership behaviors, while also being rooted in a framework that embraces the unpredictable, non-mechanistic, and non-linear VUCA world in which we now live and work.

This book offers just such a model -- a working model of contextual intelligence for leaders, managers, and decision-makers -- a practical approach to leadership in dynamic, volatile contexts. It reveals how hindsight, insight, and foresight (what I call "3D Thinking") can solve problems, and help you as a leader both fit into and understand what is going on around you, in all the contexts in which you need to function, as well as contribute.

o

This is not just a book for executives or organizational leaders; it can add value to your influence in everyday life as well. If you are a leader in a Fortune 500 company, a small church, the head of a household, or all three the contextual intelligence leadership model can help. This book teaches you how to apply contextual intelligence regardless of context and when necessary successfully transition between contexts. It can help you acquire and sustain influence with anyone, anytime, anywhere.

○

This book has a couple unique features. Following each chapter there are contemplation and critical thinking exercises that will help you integrate what was just discussed. Each chapter also provides a space for notes. Many of the concepts, stories, and illustrations are likely to invoke additional questions or thoughts. To encourage your engagement with the content I have provided space for you to write these additional thoughts and questions. So, before you read any further be sure you have a pen handy.

The book is laid out in four parts. Part 1 outlines the origins of the contextual intelligence concept. In Chapter 1 I will introduce the general concept and purpose behind contextual intelligence and in Chapter 2 describe how to assemble the contextual intelligence model, using a metaphor of a tire. In Part 2, I will delineate the three central components that are necessary to understand how the model works. In Part 3, I will discuss the 3D Thinking framework and delineate how hindsight, insight, and foresight create the structure by which the 12 contextual intelligence behaviors can be applied. Also in this part I will outline the 12 contextual intelligence behaviors and bring together all the elements of the contextual intelligence model. Finally, in Part 4, I will describe several obstacles to contextual intelligence and give recommendations to overcome those obstacles. The book is concluded with a list of actions steps that you can apply immediately as you begin to grapple with how make contextual intelligence a permanent part of how you practice leadership.

PART I

BUILDING THE CONTEXTUAL

INTELLIGENCE MODEL

- Introduction
- Overview of Contextual Intelligence

Chapter 1

INTRODUCTION

In a constantly changing world, the ability to
challenge one's mental models and explore
new ways to adapt is a competitive advantage.

-Philipp Hensler

Julie Jones was an executive for a multibillion-dollar global
company with a leading market share in its industry. Jones was
successful and well respected by her peers and those she managed. And, not incidentally, she was a skilled communicator. All
in all, her life was very gratifying -- she had achieved everything
she wanted at this stage in her career.

But because Jones had long been interested in improvement and progress, she contacted me after reading an article I'd
written about contextual intelligence. Intrigued by this concept,

she asked me to facilitate a contextual intelligence seminar at her company's headquarters, and to administer the *Contextual Intelligence Profile*™ (CIP™) to her staff.

After my seminar, Jones told me she was convinced that contextual intelligence would not only improve the work performance of her staff, it would also improve the overall quality of their lives. Contextual intelligence resonated with her as a fundamental leadership skill. And, more privately, she confided that, if she had known about it years earlier, it could have saved her first marriage.

This kind of response is what makes contextual intelligence so exciting for me. It offers a new set of tools for high-performance leadership -- your business, organization, and team will perform at higher levels if they learn to demonstrate contextual intelligence. Just as exciting, though, is its potential for increasing our happiness and satisfaction in the non-work parts of our lives. As most good leaders know, those who lead well-rounded, happy lives are usually the best performers, the ones with the most innovative and creative ideas.

○

So what *is* contextual intelligence? It can be described, simply enough, as the ability to influence anybody, in any place, at any time. It requires recognizing the dynamic variables in a situation, what behaviors are deemed important in that situation, and adjusting your behavior to exert the right influence to achieve your desired goal.

The very first time I used the term contextual intelligence, I was teaching an adult Sunday school class in the spring of 2004. I used it quite serendipitously to describe the unique skill set that the sons of Issachar used to help Israel's transition from Saul's kingdom to David's. The story is told in the Old Testament, and it describes a group of people who had the ability to accurately diagnose their context, and then use that diagnosis to make the correct decision about what to do. I thought then, as I do now, that the ability to sense or know what is going on around you is only valuable if you can leverage that information to gain a tactical advantage. In other words, understanding what goes on around you is only an asset if it helps you make better decisions.

The term, contextual intelligence, resonated in my heart and mind, and in the hearts and minds of those in that class. I began to introduce the concept in other venues and worked it into several conversations with colleagues and friends. Eventually, the term became a normal part of my conversations and discussions about leadership.

An important key to understanding contextual intelligence is the application of the two words *context* and *intelligence*. The word context originated from the Latin *contextere* and means to weave together. As a term used to describe the creation of tapestries, context is literally the interwoven and tied together fabric of a situation, which creates an intricate and unique appearance. Without context there is no meaning. Perhaps we best understand the concept of context as it relates to the enjoyment of classic literature or epic stories. As you know any good story relies on the author's ability to create context, which in turn conveys meaning about the characters and the story line.

Intelligence is a conjunction of the two Latin words, *inter* and *legere*. The first, inter, means between, and the second, legere, means to choose or read. Originally an intelligent act occurred when an individual chose correctly between two or more viable options. Of course, choosing correctly is relative, but generally the correct course of action was one that put one's self, family, or community in a better position than it had previously been. The other application of intelligence consists of one's ability to read between the lines. Reading between the lines is about understanding the meaning or implications of something that is not explicitly stated. Ultimately intelligence comes back to choosing the *best* option; and many times that choice is made after deliberating over several different opportunities any one of which might lead to an improvement over the current situation. Of course, when any of several options is an improvement the operative phrase is "best option."

By combining the concepts of context and intelligence, we arrive at the term, contextual intelligence, which literally means to accurately read between the lines then execute the best decision. This concept can be applied to any human domain – to the organizational, leadership, management, social, corporate, and personal arenas.

A few years after spontaneously using the term, contextual intelligence, in that Sunday school class, I wrote about this concept in *The Leadership Review* (winter, 2008 edition), which is a publication of the Kravis Leadership Institute at Claremont McKenna College. In that article, I expanded the concept and identified 12 competencies specific to the practice of contextual intelligence. My article was later cited in several other publications, and used as a reference when others wanted to identify the core competencies of successful leaders in uncertain and changing times.

My definition of contextual intelligence was described, for instance, as "the core competency" for nurse leaders in New Zealand; it was used to describe the skill sets required by Royal Danish Army soldiers; and it was described as a prerequisite for the prepared mind by the Dean of Dartmouth Medical School. In addition, the popular "Barefoot Guide" movement used my definition to identify the skills and abilities needed to engage the complex world of globalization.

At the same time, I regularly hear from organizations and people who are excited about the implications of contextual intelligence. It's been especially rewarding to know that some of the largest companies in the world (e.g., Procter & Gamble and Airtel, LTD.) are integrating my concept of contextual intelligence into the culture of their organizations.

○

To help you understand how the contextual intelligence model is put together, I will use a rather simple metaphor -- that of a tire. Our tire has three components: a rim, a rubber tire, and air. The rim of the tire is the central component, as it is the axis of rotation on which the tire is fitted and secured to the axle. The second component is the tire itself, and is the part that comes in contact with the road. The third component is the air that fills the tire, and is what gives it symmetry and strength.

The tire rim of our contextual intelligence model consists of three central concepts. The first concept is complexity, the second is synchronicity, and the third is tacit knowledge. I will explain each one of these concepts in detail in subsequent chapters. The tire of our contextual intelligence model is three dimensional (3D) thinking. Three-dimensional thinking is the traction of the contextual intelligence model; it grips the road and allows us to move forward. Three-dimensional thinking is the use of hindsight, insight, and foresight, when making leadership decisions, and will be described throughout the book. The air that fills the tire of the contextual intelligence model is composed of 12 empirically-based contextual intelligence competencies (behaviors), which are also discussed individually in later chapters.

This book is designed to provide a way of thinking about leadership and organizational development that is uniquely suited for the fast-paced, highly dynamic business environments that you and all leaders must now face. That way of thinking is contextual intelligence, a concept that integrates traditional leadership competencies with "non-Newtonian" theories that can help leaders function successfully in complex business environments. More specifically, these are business environments in which we encounter a leader-follower-context nexus.

Unique to the 21st century global marketplace, this nexus (or linked connection) is the way in which a leader's values and experiences converge with a follower's values and experiences – as well as with the organization's values, the social climate, and the larger culture.

In other words, unlike the relatively monodimensional business environments of the past, today's business leaders must be prepared to play a multi-dimensional game, one that takes into account a multitude of variables, in order to succeed -- to survive and thrive.

Below is a diagram Contextual Intelligence Model™ and is the basis around how this book is organized. I hope this book will prove to be a resource for you while navigating change and cultivating influence in a globally diverse marketplace.

Think 360° Exercise 1

If you could significantly improve one aspect of your life by becoming more contextually intelligent what aspect would that be and how do you envision the process unfolding?

Critical Thinking Exercise 1

Before you read any further try to clearly articulate to someone else your general understanding of what contextual intelligence is and how it might be able to help you lead or perform at a higher level.

Chapter Notes and Ideas

Chapter 2

An Overview on Contextual Intelligence

In America management is usually just a
way to make people's jobs more difficult.
                                    - Peter Drucker

Contextual intelligence is a very viable and useful model for corporate and organizational leadership. But it is much more than just a leadership model. The application of contextual intelligence influences several facets of life, which has meaningful applications for helping us to understand how behaviors and attitudes in one context are affected by or integrated into others. The best way for me to explain this is to tell the story of James Scott.

James Scott was a mid-level manager in a Fortune 500 company, and he consistently performed at such a high level that all his supervisors agreed he showed unusual potential. In fact, even though Scott had spent barely a year with the company, there was talk of promoting him to senior management.

Each time Scott spoke up in a meeting, for instance, or offered a problem-solving suggestion, he made a meaningful contribution that enhanced his reputation even more. And, in addition to all those achievements, the employees he managed and mentored not only thrived, they marveled at the wisdom he displayed beyond his years, and they credited him with helping them succeed. In a short time, Scott was handed larger and larger territories to manage, and with each successive promotion, he continued to thrive. Partly as a result of his huge success, Scott became intensely focused on cultivating and improving his leadership ability. He took many leadership courses while also consuming the best leadership books. Unfortunately, Scott developed leadership "tunnel vision" and he began to lose sight of the larger context. Ultimately, he began to exert himself in social and civic settings the same exact way he did at work. He began to believe that the exact same things that worked for him at the office would also work outside of the office, but they didn't.

Scott was greatly troubled by the fact that he didn't have the same level of influence or respect with friends and peers outside of the office as he had with supervisors and subordinates inside the office. To him, it seemed that when he demonstrated the same behaviors outside of the office that worked for him in the office he was shot down.

Eventually, Scott projected his frustration onto social peers, privately confiding to his close friends and wife that those outside of work were intentionally holding him back and sabotaging his influence. And though he continued to excel at work, he seemed unable to relate to those who had no ties to his workplace. Scott wanted everyone to see him the way that his work supervisors did. In essence, he wanted the same level of influence with social peers and friends that he enjoyed with subordinates at his company.

What Scott failed to realize was that, in spite of his good leadership skills, subordinates at work were *obligated* to follow his lead and accept his direction, while his social peers were not. At first glance, you might assume that Scott suffered from an overinflated sense of self – or some inordinate craving for power. But when I talked with him, I could tell this wasn't the case. What was wrong was, Scott had failed to diagnose his context. He couldn't understand why techniques and tactics that were so effective and even celebrated in one context failed miserably in other contexts. In fact, what I discovered was that Scott suffered from a marked lack of contextual intelligence. And so what Scott failed to realize, and his employer did not know, was that Scott's lack of contextual intelligence negatively impacted how others perceived his employer. Because Scott was having a difficult time concealing his frustration over his self-perceived lack of influence in non-work contexts, others in those non-work contexts began to wonder what his employer ever saw in him and called into question their judgment. The negative impact of this ripple effect could have led to serious consequences for Scott's company.

Scott's story may seem like a special case, but the fact is many of us suffer from contextual intelligence deficits. So what *is* contextual intelligence? Although a brief description of contextual intelligence was given earlier, here is an additional aspect of that definition which relates to Scott's situation: Contextual intelligence is the ability to recognize which behaviors are valued in any given situation, and the ability to make an intentional behavioral adjustment that "adds value" to that situation, and so garners influence within it.

In other words, contextual intelligence includes the ability to appropriately adjust your behavior, based on your diagnosis of what is important, and how it is being measured. The degree to which you can do this represents contextual intelligence. Those with low contextual intelligence are actually failing to recognize the complexity of the situational variables in which their leadership and influence operate. In fact, different contexts may require different strategies or even different skill sets.

For instance, behaviors that are deemed to be important in a specific setting will change whenever that setting changes. And it needn't be a big change; it can actually be quite subtle. A situation will be altered even when the only change is one person's departure. That person leaves with a piece of the meaning of that particular situation or context, and it will, as a result, be subtly altered. Even if the departure is short-lived, the identity of the group will change.

As leaders, it's important to pay attention to small contextual alterations that influence behaviors, attitudes, and group dynamics. This level of attention will help you in identifying those behaviors considered assets, and those behaviors considered liabilities. When you remain aware of the small changes that occur in every context, you will be able to exert influence and perform at a high level. This is why our earlier story of James Scott is significant. Scott failed to recognize that what were deemed important behaviors at work were not as important when he was not at work. And, since he had only developed the skill sets associated with what was valued at work, the skills he needed for other contexts had either atrophied or never been developed.

It's also important to note that a leader with high contextual intelligence doesn't wait for change to stop before they act. He or she intuitively knows that change *never* ends and that a disruption can occur at any moment without warning. Armed with this knowledge contextually intelligence leaders have equipped themselves to lead in the midst of a shift in context.

For example, it takes contextual intelligence to respond appropriately in the middle of a board meeting that suddenly takes a drastic turn in a different direction. We have all experienced times when everything appeared to be going smoothly and predictably in one direction to have it all suddenly derailed or turn hostile because of an ill-advised comment or off-handed remark. Responding to this sudden rise in defensiveness or entrenchment is a requirement for the job if decisions need to be made. Contextually intelligent leaders know how to manage that change intuitively based on how well they leverage hindsight, insight, and foresight (i.e., 3D Thinking).

This ability need not be daunting. It can, in fact, be exhilarating. And the exhilarating element is largely this: contextual intelligence can provide the means for responding successfully to the dynamic, complex, and constantly changing environments that we often find ourselves in. Even more exhilarating, perhaps, is the fact that we need not be born with this kind of intelligence. The behaviors associated with contextual intelligence can be objectively measured, and as a result, they can be cultivated.

○

Contextual intelligence is becoming increasingly important because leaders are casting about for answers, in a climate in which our basic assumptions about how to lead – and even what leadership is – are being challenged. And while it has always been difficult to define leadership succinctly, as the leadership role grows more complex, that difficulty only increases.

Here is why. Traditional leadership theories are insufficient for today's world because they focus solely on one of three areas: the leader, or the follower (usually in a one-on-one relationship), or the context.[71] But their singular focus does not account for the dynamic contexts that arise as soon as a leader and a follower interact. In fact, leaders and followers often collide, thereby creating a brand new context – one that needs to be navigated by both parties, and even by onlookers.

As if that weren't enough, the sheer number of leadership theories makes it difficult for leaders to decide which ones to apply, and how, and under what circumstances. Furthermore, many theories are so idiosyncratic that they are inadequate for the volatility and complexity that leaders must now navigate.[71]

Many theorists and practitioners have realized that this is a problem. And they have introduced leadership concepts based on such non-Newtonian frameworks as chaos theory,[13,71,77] complexity theory,[47,60,73] adaptive capacity,[35,75] interactional psychology,[54] and systems thinking.[30,63,64] These concepts are posited as the paradigms needed to understand how organizations and leaders can thrive in volatile environments within a global economy. In other words, they provide the perspective required for leadership in today's context-rich environments.

Unfortunately, many of these concepts fall short in providing a usable model (one with measurable competencies) for practitioners. Leadership theories that incorporate non-Newtonian concepts like complexity theory and chaos theory must -- in order to be useful -- include the competencies that need to inform the behavior that leads to proficiency.

Contextual intelligence answers this need by extending complexity-based leadership models (through the integration of tacit knowledge, synchronicity, and time orientation -- explanations of these will follow), and offering leaders the kind of outcome that immediately impacts performance.

Here is a list of some of the benefits associated with practicing contextual intelligence, which can provide:

- An understanding of why success may occur in one context while failure occurs in another (see the James Scott story above)

- A reduction in conflict, and an increasing awareness of values – both your own and others' values
- A growing ability to effectively influence others regardless of context
- An ability to respond well and to profit from change
- An increase in team buy-in
- An increasing ability to contribute sooner in a new context, or after a context changes
- An appreciation of both external and internal influences on a context

○

And so, to briefly reiterate: The overall context in which leaders are now required to operate is profoundly different from the one they might have encountered one or two decades ago. So what is needed is a correspondingly drastic change in the perception of leadership. Especially as the basic assumptions underlying much of what is still taught in the realm of both organizational and leadership practices are out of date.[55]

In our current complex business environment, knowledge is fast becoming the core commodity, and the rapid production of knowledge is fundamental to survival.[5] But traditional leadership theories were developed long before the "knowledge economy" came to dominate, and so it is long past time for an entirely new conceptual model of leadership.[51] Contextual Intelligence provides that model and outlines the corresponding competencies to help make it actionable.

Think 360⁰ Exercise 2

What are the metrics or standards that are used to determine success in the different areas of your life?

Critical Thinking Exercise 2

How accurately do you currently diagnose the values of the people and groups to whom you relate or belong?

Chapter Notes and Ideas

PART II

CENTRAL CONCEPTS OF
CONTEXTUAL INTELLIGENCE

- Introduction to Part II
- Non-Newtonian Systems
- Synchronicity
- Tacit-based Learning

Introduction to Part II

To take full advantage of the contextual intelligence model -- and what it can do for you as a leader, as well as what it can do for the people in your organization – it's important to understand the three central aspects of contextual intelligence. As mentioned in Chapter 1, they can be compared to the rim of a tire, in that they are the axis of rotation around which the contextual intelligence model moves. These three aspects are:

- Complexity theory (or Non-Newtonian thinking)
- Synchronicity
- Tacit knowledge

Figure 1: Central Aspects (Tire Rim) of the Contextual Intelligence Model

Unless you apply the contextual intelligence model with an understanding of what the three central elements are -- and how they relate to the bigger picture -- contextual intelligence cannot give you the forward momentum you seek, since they represent the "tire rim" that makes movement possible.

Chapter 3

Non-Newtonian Thinking

It isn't that they can't see the solution. It's
that they can't see the problem.
                    -G.K. Chesterton

Consider Alan and Linda, administrators at the same college in a prestigious university. Alan acquired a wealth of experience from a variety of different industries before entering academia, and has a keen sense of the three central aspects of contextual intelligence. For example, he sees the world as complex and understands the dynamic of relationships that exist between people within an organization, and that exist between people and the organization. In other words, Alan realizes that people influence the organizational culture and the organizational culture influences people, in turn. Alan appreciates and even tries to discover the external influences and outliers that shape what he and others perceive. So he understands that problems cannot be solved by removing a "problem" person or by hiring the "right" person. For Alan, solutions are simple: study the relationships between people and the organization; then redefine, recalibrate, and realign those relationships.

Linda, on the other hand, who also has decades of experience -- but all of it within academia -- views the world as complicated. For her, everything can be isolated and has a direct and measurable cause and effect. Consequently, she believes that every problem can be reduced to its smallest component and, once identified, that part can be fixed and reinserted into the whole. In other words, if there is a problem, identify who or what the problem is, remove it, and the problem is solved. Linda is often heard saying, "It's not personal, it's business." As a result, she only sees problems; constantly isolates people; and puts everyone into one of two groups – those that are for, and those that are against. To complicate things further, Linda has a difficult time understanding why the consideration of external variables is important. In her mind, outliers are not relevant. In fact, her entire academic career has been built on the strategy of making decisions by eliminating outliers and using averages.

Consequently, even if these two agree on a course of action, their approach to problem solving is completely different. Alan has a non-Newtonian view, whereas Linda has a Newtonian view. This means that Alan sees people as the primary asset and allows them to be active contributors to how the organization functions. On the other hand, Linda sees the organization (the system) as the primary asset and people as a means to sustain the organization. As a result, Linda is always to trying to "honor the system" by maintaining the status quo, promoting the organization, and keeping power and resources evenly balanced. She lives by the mantra, "If it ain't broke, don't fix it." Alan, on the other hand, actively looks for things to change, promotes people, and distributes power and resources to those who are using it most effectively.

Keeping in mind that both Alan and Linda are very capable managers, if leaders are defined by whether or not they have followers, who of these two is the leader? Because Alan understands the unstable nature of how people and organizations are constantly impacting each other, he is the real leader. You see, Alan has a non-Newtonian worldview.

In order to understand what a Non-Newtonian paradigm is, we need to briefly look back at the earlier Newtonian paradigm. The primary tenant of this long-popular worldview rests upon a notion of the world as not only law-abiding, stable, and mechanistic, but one with predictable outcomes. As you might expect, Newtonian-based physics relies on laws and rules that never change.

The Newtonian-based paradigm has enjoyed popularity because it offers a view of the world as comfortably predictable, stable, and orderly. Historically, organizational and leadership behaviors have been based on a Newtonian understanding that all things work in accordance with known patterns. And while it's true that certain Newtonian-based laws are well established in our physical world (the law of gravity), with the advent of quantum physics, as well as recent discoveries regarding the functioning of biological systems, such Newtonian-based concepts as equilibrium, homeostasis, and predictability have been called into question.

Concomitantly, scholars and practitioners have recently introduced non-Newtonian-based leadership paradigms as a way of understanding leadership -- in what Bob Johansen, author of *Leaders Make the Future* and Distinguished Fellow at the Institute for the Future, has dubbed a VUCA (Volatile, Uncertain, Complex, Ambiguous) world. Two of the most important non-Newtonian-based paradigms recently introduced into the leadership field are chaos theory and complexity theory. Let's take a brief look at both.

CHAOS THEORY

Chaos theory offers an alternative to Newton's mechanistic view of the physical world by proposing the alternate view that not all processes can be pre-determined or are easily recognized. Indeed, the obvious problem with viewing life in a linear manner is that it blinds us to "life processes," those unanticipated formative events that occur throughout the lives of companies, as well as in our own lives.[77] However, chaos theory implies, as a casualty of its name, randomness and disorganization. But, as it turns out, chaos is in actuality patterned and not disorganized at all. So what ends up being labeled as "chaos" is actually anything for which the underlying patterns have not yet been recognized. If we take the time to look more closely or change our perspective most of what we call chaos is actually patterned.

As a result, while chaos theory describes the non-linear and unpredictable, it does so by recognizing that what appears to be chaotic is actually patterned. For example, think back to a moment when someone's reaction was disproportionate to your action. You may have wondered why your minor infraction resulted in a major eruption. On the other hand, you may remember times when you did something that would seem really annoying, but the same person hardly noticed. These unpredictable responses are an example of chaos theory at work, because even though they appear random, they actually follow a predictable pattern. And here it is.

Most people have a threshold of tolerance for behavior they consider irresponsible. Each infraction they are confronted with consumes a certain amount of their tolerance, and at some point, all their tolerance is used up and an "overreaction" occurs.

For instance, assume your boss has a tolerance threshold of ten units, and five weeks ago you neglected to put staples in the copier room stapler after using them all up, and that cost you one unit. Not a big deal. What you didn't realize is that you only have nine units left. Two weeks later, you made a huge mistake that cost eight units. But after a slap on the wrist, all was forgiven – though you then had just one unit left. Yesterday, you made a very minor mistake, one similar to forgetting to refill the stapler, but you got yelled at by your boss and reassigned to a job below your pay grade. What just happened is not random at all, nor is it discrimination, or anything else. It is perfectly understandable, but only if you're not looking for predictable patterns, and instead realize that what appears random actually hides within it an "invisible" pattern.

Chaos theory offers more than just an explanation for what seems, on the surface, chaotic. But to understand its other benefits, we need to explore three of its "sub-concepts" -- namely, strange attractors, phase transition, and double-loop learning.

Strange Attractors

Strange attractors are the unidentified influencers of patterned movement.[13] In the quantum realm, they refer to an unknown phenomenon that is continually pulling matter toward itself.[80] And so, in spite of apparent randomness, this implies that there is something ordering that movement -- or, at the very least, causing a convergence of unrelated phenomenon (the presence of strange attractors will also help us conceptualize synchronicity, which we'll discuss a bit later).

One example of a strange attractor is the personal conviction that everything will ultimately work itself out, or that everything happens for a reason. Understanding this aspect of chaos theory provides one reason for the feeling of peace that sometimes occurs in the middle of a stressful experience. Because feeling peacefulness seems at odds with stress, strange attractors account for it by recognizing that we can "pull matter toward ourselves," or pull peacefulness into our emotional landscape by *wanting* to feel peaceful. A strange attractor is a hidden, behind-the-scenes force that pulls something out of apparent chaos – from something that is unrecognizable – into something that *is* recognizable. It may be as simple as the way a store owner manages frustration with an obnoxious customer by reminding himself that "the customer is always right."

Typically the strange attractors in our lives are underlying core beliefs or core values which motivate our outlook and behavior, but reside under the surface of our conscience awareness. These strange attractors can have a profound effect on the organizations where we work, the social networks where we play, as well as our families and civic responsibilities.

Phase Transition

Another sub-concept within chaos theory is phase transition. Before an unseen pattern can be identified, there is an awkward moment when the pattern is blurry because it is in the process of taking shape and is not yet fully formed. So we might say that phase transition is the place between stability and anarchy,[66] or the unstable state that exists between stable states – the phase between ice and water,[32] for instance, or to use our store owner again, the phase between his frustration and its relinquishment. But frustration isn't something that he can instantly turn off like a light switch. There is a gradual transition – a point when he is neither frustrated nor calm. The fact is that there is a middle place between these two feelings. Most people do not have a name for this middle place, or worse expect the transition to be instant. Because we are not aware of the fact that a "middle place" is a normal part of the process our default is anxiety in the midst of what we consider chaos. Fortunately the middle place does have a name and it is called phase transition and it is real and must be accounted for.

Perhaps this illustration will help. I often tell people that life is more about navigating hallways than it is walking through doors. What I mean is that most people assume life's great moments are when we seize an opportunity or successfully execute a plan. Therefore, everyone is always looking for the next opportunity or new idea – they are trying to open a door. What we fail to recognize is that doors have spaces between them – hallways. Most hallways are longer and darker than we want. Before you can walk through any door you must successfully navigate the hallway. Life is typically not one door right after the other. In the grand scheme there are more hallways to navigate than doors to open. Phase transition is akin to the hallway. Your previous idea and your new idea are the two doors and phase transition is the hallway between them. When you embrace the idea that hallways are an important aspect of the journey it can help by making what once appeared to be chaotic more manageable.

Organizationally, phase transition is uncomfortable. It means moving into a temporary stage of ambiguous identity without knowing what new identity the transition will eventually bring about. A bureaucratic organization wishing to become a learning organization will undergo phase transition, for instance, before realizing its goal.[50] In other words, there will be a time during the transition when its identity is neither bureaucratic nor that of a learning organization. Functioning during this time of ambiguity may require a skill set that may not be common to either bureaucratic or learning organizations, but knowing what to do in a time of transition is extremely valuable. Largely, that means knowing that there is solace in the realization that, even though the length of this transitional phase is un-known, it can be endured because of the anticipated desirable outcome.

Double-Loop Learning

Double-loop (adaptive) learning is the third sub-concept within chaotic systems that we'll look at, and it lets us assess how well we are performing in a specific context, and modify our behav-ior, accordingly.[13] This kind of learning is akin to what Richard Paul, Chair of the National Council for Excellence in Critical Thinking, describes as thinking about your thinking, while you're thinking, in order to change your thinking. It essentially requires that you analyze and correct your own words or thoughts as they occur.

Double-loop learning necessitates being tuned into sud-den changes in our environment, including our perceptions and those of others. In short, double-loop learning engages us in the process of diagnosing contextual variables while they are hap-pening, in order to address - rather than merely bandage - a core issue. In essence, double-loop learning requires reconsidering our governing beliefs when faced with a problem we can't seem to solve.

For example, we all have been faced with experiences that contradict what we have always believed to be true – what I call crises of experience. This is when belief tells you one thing, but experience tells you something different. Double-loop learn-ing helps you manage the crises of experience by offering you an opportunity to consider alternate solution(s) by taking on a new perspective.

Here is how it can work. Let's assume a founding CEO is trying to breathe life into his dying organization. He assumes that he needs "young blood" with new and fresh ideas. So he brings on new and younger management, but the organization is still suffering. He tries a more drastic intervention and asked his new staff to rewrite old and outdated policies, but that doesn't do it either. Finally out of desperation he steps down as CEO, restricting himself to the participation on the board, leaving day to day operations to the new CEO. Still, the organization is struggling to revive. What should this CEO do next? So far our CEO has tried three different single-loop solutions.

Single-loop learning (Figure 2) is a one-way cycle between action and consequence that looks like this: apply a solution and see what happens; if a solution didn't take, apply another solution and see what happens; keep repeating until a solution takes. What this CEO has failed to do is evaluate his governing belief. A belief that assumes organizational vitality depends solely on leadership and management. By challenging this governing belief he may open his organization up to the possibility that other factors influence organizational momentum – other factors like the economy, competitor's market share, his company's product offerings, or stakeholder's values. If one of these is true no amount of organizational restructuring will help. Of course other scenarios are also possible, maybe his governing belief is that the world needs his organization or that no one else can do what his does. Regardless governing beliefs need to be challenged.

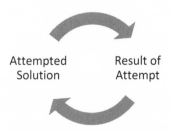

Attempted   Result of
Solution   Attempt

Figure 2: Single-Loop Learning

Double-loop learning takes place when an attempted solution fails. Instead of trying a different solution, or the same solution with a new twist, it is necessary to reconsider what we were trying to accomplish in the first place (our governing belief). Contextually intelligent leaders inherently gravitate toward a double-loop learning process. They are predisposed to evaluating their (and other's) governing beliefs before offering a solution.

Mary directed a large department staffed by highly trained professionals, so her department outperformed many other departments within her company. Her department had four divisions, but they were extremely unstable and competed among themselves. This meant that, when the department as a whole needed the four divisions to collaborate, hostilities erupted among them. Mary repeatedly tried to solve the "lack of unity" problem by changing division leaders, or by taking other actions she considered "baby steps" (making meetings more amicable by changing policies or reducing the number of meetings to decrease face-to-face interaction). More drastic measures included hiring a new division leader whenever the old leader was unsuccessful at changing the culture of his division, but it never worked. The division's culture never changed and the hostility and competition between people and divisions grew worse.

Mary decided to seek out my advice, and after describing one particularly hostile department meeting, it struck me that she had fallen into a single-loop learning cycle. Mary needed to break out of this single-loop cycle, by reconsidering the governing belief she'd learned in her MBA program, which was that leaders create culture and changing leaders was the only way to change a division's culture. By asking her to examine this situation from a double-loop perspective, instead, she soon had two revelations: 1) Her governing belief was not proven by her experience; 2) Her division leaders were not the source of the problem. Fortunately, Mary was able to improve her department's morale and implement a better organizational structure, and this proved to be the real change her department needed.

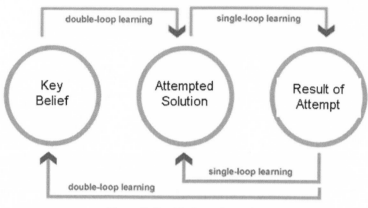

Figure 3: Double-Loop Learning

Chaos theory offers the understanding that life is patterned even when it appears disorganized. It also provides "sub-understandings," one of which is an awareness of what influences the patterned movement behind seemingly disparate things, or what are called strange attractors. Another sub-understanding within chaos theory, phase transition, offers the reassurance that the unknown identity an organization assumes while changing into something else is temporary, but still requires different strategies of interaction. And finally, the third sub-understanding, double-loop learning, defines the process of making behavioral adjustments in real time, based on a good hard look at what beliefs govern your choice of solutions, rather than after the fact (which could be too late).

COMPLEXITY THEORY

Complexity theory offers organizational leadership insights that fit the ongoing major global transition from bureaucratic (industrial-driven) organizations to organizations that are knowledge-driven (organic).[73] One of the main drivers behind how complexity theory can be integrated into contextual intelligence is the concept of adaptive capacity, put forth by Ronald Heifetz, founder of the Center for Public Leadership at the John F. Kennedy School of Government at Harvard University. Adaptive capacity is the ability to meet the fluid demands of each situation by mobilizing people with different needs and backgrounds to think differently. In other words, it means getting people who normally might not agree, or who have completely divergent experiences, to think from the perspective of someone else.

Applying contextual intelligence through the lens of adaptive capacity requires realizing how you are being influenced by, and how you are influencing, the situation, and it asks that you think differently. To achieve the ability to think differently, the first step is to understand the differences between something that is complex and something that is complicated -- a more than just semantic difference.[73]

Complicated Systems

Complicated systems are typically closed systems which contain a large number of independent parts (stakeholders, employees, vendors, customers, shareholders, and so forth). At the same time, they can be understood by breaking them into their smallest parts and studying those small parts. As a closed (internal) system, a complicated context has no need to consider external variables. Furthermore, when problem-solving in a complicated system, all the necessary parts for a solution are inherent within the system itself. The reason is, everything relevant to the system is contained within it, and so decisions can be based on averages. Stated another way, outliers are not accounted for, and they are often excluded from consideration, much of the way Linda (in our earlier example) approached problem solving.

One simple example of a complicated system is a watch, something with many moving parts, all contained inside the watch case. If it needs repairing, it can be disassembled down to its smallest component parts; broken parts can be replaced; and it can be reassembled into working order. The parts of a watch, though detailed and many, are very systematic and reproducible, and are easy to understand. All you need is expertise in watch making, and no problem is too big.

Applying this ideology to leadership, if everything in an organization can be broken into its smallest component parts, we simply need to learn all there is to know about the organization's parts, and no problem is too big. If anything breaks, we can take it apart and fix it. We like organizations that have simple component parts, because they are easy to fix when they break - as long as we have the expertise. This is why we love to think of everything as complicated; when something is complicated, it's easy to fix; we take it apart, find and replace the broken piece(s), and reassemble.

For example, say an organization has a problem with a customer. If it is a complicated system, we reduce the problem down to its smallest component part – the customer – bring in the customer service expert to fix that customer's problem, and move on. Everyone is happy. When the same or a similar problem occurs the next day with a different customer, we repeat the process. This is single-loop problem solving, based on a complicated system, and we love it.

Another reason why we love to see the world as complicated is because so much of the information we use on a daily basis, even subconsciously, has been acquired through the scientific method. The scientific method (also known as empiricism or empirical science) is rooted in a process based on complicated systems, and it requires the following sequential steps:

1. Ask a question
2. Find background information
3. Construct a hypothesis
4. Test that hypothesis
5. Analyze the data and draw a conclusion
6. Communicate the results

We trust the outcome of this process, and are biased against anything that cannot be empirically tested. This is the epitome of problem solving from a complicated systems framework. Unfortunately, we live in a complex system and not a complicated system. Complex systems function in a completely different way than complicated systems do, and they require a different intervention for solving problems.

Complex Systems

Complex systems have many related parts and are open to outside influences. And so, in order to understand them, we need to have an understanding of how interdependent all the parts are. This demands an internal and external analysis. For example, in a complex system our earlier customer problem cannot be isolated to a single customer, nor is a customer service expert the only needed intervention. In a complex system, the problem of a single customer should be recognized as a symptom of a larger issue. Therefore, the solution transcends simply addressing the customer's complaint, although that is necessary, it requires an organization-wide assessment. An assessment that may find out that the source of the customer's problem has little to do with this customer. Therefore, the customer service expert becomes a smaller part of a larger team that is assembled to address both the customer's problem and the larger systemic problem. For example, an incompetent or grumpy employee may be the source of the customer's complaint; but replacing that employee may only be a temporary solution for a larger issue. That larger issue may be poor hiring practices, poor evaluation practices, or an inadequate corporate training program.

Furthermore, complex systems, unlike complicated ones, are highly sensitive to "small perturbations."[49] Perturbations are external forces that cause something to become unsettled because they bumped into it. In a complex system, it is possible for seemingly unrelated components to bump into one another, causing a chain reaction of unpredictable change.[73] But there's more. Any resulting change usually occurs where it is least expected, and as history cannot be revisited, the trajectory of that change cannot be altered.[21] In other words, change that results from a small perturbation does not always occur in the obvious spot.

Because the trajectory of these changes cannot be predicted or changed, outliers – those influences or factors that fall outside of the average – can have a profound impact on the organization. If the squeaky wheel gets the grease, then the outliers are the squeaky wheel. Therefore, outliers are also treated differently in a complex system. In complex systems, outliers are always significant actors that create perceptible outcomes. Within a complexity-based mindset, the failure to consider outliers in the grand scheme of things could be a fatal mistake. For example, if we asked the New Orleans levee engineers to consider outliers -- instead of going with the law of averages -- the damage from Hurricane Katrina might have been minimized.

As you can see, handling problems, opportunities, and decision-making within a complex system requires a completely different way of thinking and a different kind of intelligence – one that embraces complexity and enables us to diagnose the context. Here are the main differences between complicated and complex systems, in Table 1, below:

A Complicated System	A Complex System
• Has many independent parts	• Has many related parts
• Eliminates outliers as irrelevant	• View outliers as meaningful
• Is closed and unresponsive to outside influences	• Is open and responsive to outside influences
• Views solving problems as complicated and requiring the intervention of specialists	• Views solving problems is simple -- anyone can do it
• Isolates and quarantines problems so no one finds out	• Accounts for the holistic impact of problems
• Has component parts extracted and analyzed individually, apart from the whole	• Has component parts that have a symbiotic relationship with other parts, and which cannot be analyzed in isolation

These differences mean that leadership within a complex system (your organization is a complex system within a larger complex system) is a behavioral requirement of everyone. Always remember that in complexity-based frameworks, leadership is not relegated to those in executive-level hierarchal positions.

The implications of these and other non-Newtonian paradigms for contextual intelligence are far reaching, as they refine how organized systems are perceived - both internally by employees, and externally by interested onlookers. And, as we'll soon see, those implications also include how leaders deal with, and understand, the past; anticipate the future; and place a priority on the present. Finally - because in a complex system anyone can influence everything - they include a profound impact on our ideas concerning who a leader is, or can be; how leadership is measured; and where leadership takes place.

Think 360^0 Exercise 3

What are the strange attractors in your life?

Ask a close friend to help you identify different phase transitions that occurred during your professional development.

Critical Thinking Exercise 3

How have outliers affected your decision making regarding key decisions in your life?

Chapter Notes and Ideas

CHAPTER 4

SYNCHRONICITY

The greatest danger in times of turbulence is
not the turbulence; it is to act with yesterday's logic.

                    - Peter Drucker

Synchronicity, the second of three concepts that contribute to
the effective practice of contextual intelligence, is a term coined
by the renowned psychotherapist, Carl Jung. Jung coined the
term after an astonishing coincidence that occurred with a ther-
apy patient. After his patient finished describing a rare beetle
that had appeared in her dream, there was an unrelenting tap-
ping at the window. Jung went to see what it was. Amazingly
enough, the culprit turned out to be the same kind of beetle his
patient had just described. This meaningful coincidence gave
Jung the idea for a word describing two or more events that are

not causally related but that occur coincidentally – thus resulting in a meaningful connection. The term he chose was *synchronicity*. His concept was later expanded to include connected events that may not have occurred simultaneously or consecutively. Meaning that it is possible a second event could occur much later, which would trigger the recall of the initial event and then at that point assign meaning to it. Thus it is possible that meaning can be assigned to an event well after it occurred.

As leaders, we may not notice events that might trigger an insight, because we tend to look for cause-and-effect relationships, and these distract us from seeing meaningful synchronous relationships. But Peter Senge, author of *The Fifth Discipline: The Art & Practice of the Learning Organization*, suggests that opportunities for significant change often arise through synchronous, though not necessarily connected, processes that produce a "meaningful coincidence" and other synergies. A synchronous experience occurs when we recognize that two or more events connect in a meaningful way, but they are not causally related (necessarily). In other words, it is remembering and connecting events from your personal history of experiences.

The application of synchronicity requires recalling lessons learned or meaningful events from experiences, either as they happen or from the past. An example in the present would be that of a small business owner making a very difficult decision which will negatively impact the financial stability of her employees, but as she contemplates this decision, she looks out her office window and sees an employee's wife and young children walking into the office building. At that moment, she realizes it would be a mistake to put her employees' financial security at risk. Based on that moment of synchronicity, she changes the trajectory of her decision and, ultimately, the company. In retrospect, it was the right decision and in that moment of clarity an easy one to make. So capitalizing on the synergy between apparently unrelated experiences may provide a tacit-based framework, one in which ideas are generated more easily and leadership capacity is elevated.

Since we now recognize that we live in a complex, ever-changing world (we always have, we just haven't always recognized it), the application of synchronicity is highly relevant as, in one sense, it involves the refusal to see anything as extraneous -- as irrelevant. (This doesn't mean that everything has a meaning, however, as looking for meaning where none exists can be unwise.) But synchronicity underscores the fact that experience outside a given context may have applicability. The practice of synchronicity requires openness to the idea that knowledge gained in one context can be applied to a completely unrelated context. Take, for instance, how we use our memories of when and where we learned something.

Most of us don't forget what we've learned, as much as we forget where we stored that information. What happens, as we learn lessons throughout our lifetime is that we store them in context-specific parts of their brain. So when we learn something at work we typically only use that knowledge at work. Because the experience that facilitated the learning occurred in a specific context, our minds code and store it as information relevant to that context. This explains why we may repeat mistakes when we encounter the same situation in a different setting, or with different people.

One useful way to leverage synchronicity, however, is to be intentional about where your mind files knowledge. In other words, when you learn something at work, don't limit yourself to using it at work. Make all your experiences, and the knowledge you gained from them, relevant and accessible, regardless of the context in which that learning occurred. Take, for instance, our earlier example of the small business owner contemplating a decision to sacrifice the financial stability of her employees for a potential opportunity. Earlier, she decided against it based on seeing the young family of an employee walk into her building. Now imagine that she decides against it because of a spontaneous flashback to her childhood when she witnessed an argument between her parents over how tight money was. Based on that memory, all sorts of things could be going through her mind about why not to put the financial security of her employees at risk, none of which have anything to do with the reality of her present situation. In this sense synchronicity is very meaningful and can contribute significantly to applying contextual intelligence.

Tacit-based learning, the third concept that contributes to the effective practice of contextual intelligence, and which we'll look at next, has a reciprocal relationship with synchronicity. Together, they can be catalysts for developing a framework for leadership that responds well in a fast-paced, change-oriented, and dynamic context.

Think 360⁰ Exercise 4

Take a moment to consider all the different times synchronicity (as described by Carl Jung) has happened in your life, and how have those times influenced your decisions.

Critical Thinking Exercise 4

What life experiences have you discarded as irrelevant to your professional development?

Chapter Notes and Ideas

Chapter 5

Tacit-Based Learning

The person who knows "how" will always
have a job. The person who knows "why" will
always be the boss.

- Diane Ravitch

The actions of a skillful leader are largely based on tacit knowledge,[2] the third concept that contributes to the effective practice of contextual intelligence. Tacit knowledge is often described as intuition or wisdom. Tacit knowledge is action oriented, typically acquired without direct or intentional help from others, and enables us to achieve our goals.[68,69] Tacit knowledge is what you know to be true, but cannot articulate how you learned it. Consequently, tacit knowledge is difficult to teach ("Some things are better caught than taught") and this is partly why it has long been the domain of experts.

Several years ago, a friend of mine told me a story that is a perfect example of tacit knowledge. Frank (my friend) was a clinical liaison for new physicians completing a sports medicine rotation, and he recalled a particular physician standing next to him while they both observed an injury occurring on the field. Within seconds of the athlete falling to the ground, Frank matter-of-factly said to the physician, "He just tore his ACL." (Anterior Cruciate Ligament) But the doctor doubted my friend's diagnosis, and said, "There's no way you can know that."

The next day, an MRI confirmed Frank's diagnosis -- that the injured athlete did indeed have an ACL tear. The doctor turned to Frank and, in disbelief, asked, "How did you know his ACL was torn?" Frank's response wasn't quite what the physician had in mind. "I don't know," he said, "I just knew."

Some people would have called it instinct, or intuition, or a lucky guess, but Frank recalls being very confident. In other words, he knew that he knew. And because Frank made an assessment based on tacit knowledge, he didn't know how or why he knew. Jack Welch, the retired CEO of General Electric, refers to this phenomenon as "leading from the gut."

Researchers believe that most of our decisions, regardless of context, are based on tacit knowledge. That is why, when we're asked why we did something a certain way, we often reply, "I don't know."

Our tacit understanding comes from two sources: experience and analogical reasoning.[83] In its simplest form, the best source of tacit knowledge is trial-and-error experience. And if we want to speed the development of our tacit knowledge, we should make decisions based on associations between attempted actions and resulting outcomes, whether positive or negative. Stated even more simply, tacit knowledge is the result of learning from our mistakes (and those of others). In fact, experience enhances performance only when it is transformed into tacit knowledge, and that is possible only when we are able to analyze our actions and decisions in light of real outcomes.[25] This means we have to believe that consequences matter. So we should be intentional about analyzing the outcomes and consequences of our behavior and attitudes at all times, and in every circumstance.

One way to apply this is to begin realizing that every experience - and every outcome of an action - is an opportunity to learn. Nothing is more pompous than a leader who thinks he already knows how to do something and, as a result, won't evaluate or consider new ways to behave. Once you have embraced the idea that every experience contains one or more teachable moments, the next step is to intentionally critique every learning experience by asking yourself the following questions:

1. What did I just learn?
2. Does what I just learned confirm or challenge previous assumptions?
3. Where else can I apply the lesson I just learned?

Every time you experience a consequence from an action, whether good or bad, critique it in the above manner.

ANALOGICAL REASONING

Analogical reasoning is a significant source of tacit knowledge.[83] This is because you are creating an analogy from an experience in the past and applying it to an unrelated situation in the present. When analogical reasoning is used appropriately, it makes up for a lack of direct experience with a given situation, as analogical reasoning helps you compare apparent similarities between the two situations. By using analogical reasoning, you can recognize a trend in a given context, even if you have never experienced that context before.

The irony of analogical reasoning is that it requires making judgments about new situations based on experience you haven't had, or based on unrelated experiences. The best leaders and top performers in uncertain times have an uncanny ability to do this. They tend to see connections, corollaries, and parallels between people, places, things, and events that most people do not. Often, this is because of an inclination toward analogical reasoning.

Analogical reasoning is the next best thing to actually having been there. It draws on other (unrelated or forgotten) experiences, and finds reasonable comparisons to variables influencing the present situation. This is an incredibly important skill to develop, especially in dynamic and changing environments. Because change occurs so fast and so often, we need to merge the lessons learned from unrelated experiences. This process is similar to synchronicity, but not exactly the same. For example, you may not have a direct experience with mergers and acquisitions and how to integrate employees from two different organizations, but you do remember your first day of school in a new town (or perhaps you have a blended family and can remember the stress and trauma of having a new stepsister). Imagine that a merger of two companies is something like these experiences and use those memories to inform your actions. That is analogical reasoning.

The more experiences you have in disparate arenas, the greater your capacity to create accurate analogies. As a result, it really is possible to develop your capacity for analogical reasoning. And, as you might expect, the best way to facilitate analogical reasoning is by increasing your exposure to new phenomena and experience. Bob Johansen, the author of *Leaders Make the Future: Ten New Leadership Skills for an Uncertain World*, has called this "immersion learning" -- by which he means actively engaging in activities you've never done before. Immersion learning not only facilitates analogical reasoning, it adds to your reservoir of experience, which in turn contributes to your intuition and wisdom.

Wisdom

Michael Polanyi, one of the world's foremost experts on the theory of knowledge, discusses tacit knowledge as a core component of wisdom, a concept rooted in the ability to extract and organize our experience. In a sense, wisdom could be seen as a way to measure our tacit knowledge. Achieving wisdom requires a balance between the interests of self and those of stakeholders, relative to the needs of a given context. So wisdom requires the correct application of experience, while simultaneously considering inter–personal, intra-personal, and extra-personal values, in a complex mix of relationships. This means that wisdom is best recognized when a solution satisfies multiple stakeholders, without asking anyone to compromise and silences opposition.

For many people, wisdom is simply the elusive ability to say and do the right thing at the right time. But wisdom does not have to be elusive. By intentionally engaging every aspect of life as it happens (in other words, don't wait until an experience is over to evaluate it), and organizing the knowledge gained from experiences in a way that makes it quickly accessible, we can become wiser.

How can we do that? One way is by recognizing that it's much easier to make our experiences accessible if every one of them is considered valuable (at least initially). The wisest among us learn valuable lessons from the consequences of every experience the first time it happens. But those who do not typically need a much longer time to develop wisdom. Every society has a name for people who do not learn from their experiences, ours calls them fools. The only way to assess if someone has learned from an experience is to put him in the same or a similar situation, and see if he makes the same or a similar mistake. Mistakes are not bad, all mistakes can become priceless learning experiences, but repeating mistakes – well, that *is* bad.

FIRSTHAND AND VICARIOUS EXPERIENCE

To accurately evaluate your context, two types of experience are needed. The first is vicarious experience, and the second is firsthand experience.[7]

Vicarious Experience

"Joe is living vicariously through his children." Reading that sentence, you understand that Joe uses his kids to bring new meaning to his life. In other words, he wishes he were young, active, and healthy again. When we live vicariously through the lives of others (or through movies and books), we may temporarily feel what it is like to be someone else. And, for many of us, this is simply an escape from the pressures of our own lives. But vicarious experiences can have more productive uses.

Contextual intelligence makes use of vicarious experience as a means of learning appropriate new behaviors, because it requires empathy. Merely wanting to replicate someone's success, or avoid that person's failure, is not enough. We need to embrace the lessons they learned, as the judicious use of vicarious experience can be a tremendous asset when firsthand experience is not available.

For example, King Solomon, believed by many – religious and non-religious alike - to be the wisent man who ever lived, observed the way that ants accomplish all that they do with no designated leader, and he applied it to human organizations. Combining the concepts of vicarious experiences, synchronicity, and analogical reasoning, he concluded the ants can teach us a thing or two about productivity and leadership.

Ants have garnered a lot of press attention, of late, as an example of the adaptive capacity of a complex system. There are even architects who mimic ant mounds in their designs because of the cooling efficiency that ant structures demonstrate. But, for you, there is a choice. You could either complete an MBA program and discover, as a result, how complex systems mimic the behavior of ants, *or* you could use vicarious experience and apply the observation of a man who lived 3000 years ago. Isn't it easier, more cost effective, and efficient to do the latter – a technique that also translates into wisdom?

Firsthand Experience

Because engaging in vicarious experiences isn't always possible and can be emotionally draining, we may decide that seeking out firsthand experience is what's needed. For example, a friend might have told us about the epiphany he had while climbing Mt. Kilimanjaro. And, instead of vicariously embracing his epiphany, we decide to climb that mountain, too – hoping for a similar experience. Alas, our experience is completely different. And while we now have a firsthand experience of our own, we missed the chance to *also* learn what our friend has learned.

Applying Vicarious and Firsthand Experience
Understanding how you relate to others within rapidly changing contexts is a necessary skill, if you want to move effectively be-

tween contexts that are uncertain, complex, and ambiguous. In such contexts, learning from vicarious experience is critical to performing well, because it shortens the proverbial learning curve. So it is a good idea to gain wisdom from vicarious experiences by using analogical reasoning.

One other reason why this is so important is that the scope of firsthand learning is typically -- unless intentionally changed -- restricted to the context in which it was learned. But tacit knowledge can be applied in any situation, at any time, in any place, and there is no restriction on when, where, or how it is applied[76] -- or even if it should be applied. This fact helps us value what we gain through vicarious experience, analogical reasoning, and synchronicity, even more.

When discussing different types of experience and the formation of wisdom, the concept of innovation often emerges. It may not be obvious at first, but innovation is related to analogical reasoning. Innovative and creative ideas, consistently great performance, knowledge management, and their requisite behaviors are at an all-time premium. So leveraging different types of experience and using tacit knowledge, synchronicity, and analogical reasoning to enhance the ability to be innovative is vital.

INNOVATION

Consider this question, "What are you doing when you have your best ideas?" By which I mean ideas that solve problems, ideas that are truly creative. Most of us would say, "I'm in the shower." Or "I'm mowing the lawn." Or "I'm driving home." Most of our best ideas arrive when they are least expected, and rarely when we are being paid to have them.

Researchers and practitioners have long understood that the key to innovation lies in that much-maligned and overused cliché, "thinking outside the box." This proverbial box is the context, the parameters surrounding a finite number of specialized experiences. Often, we relegate our experiences and the things we learned from them to the boxes (contexts) in which we learned them. Ironically, most of our attempts to go outside the box usually end up taking us to another box. But when we *are* able to draw from experience outside the current context, there tends to be an increase in novel and useful ideas.

Each of the previous ideas, synchronicity, analogical reasoning, first-hand and vicarious experiences lead to becoming aware of tacit knowledge, which informs our decisions. When we become aware of how tacit knowledge informs our decision making innovation becomes easier.

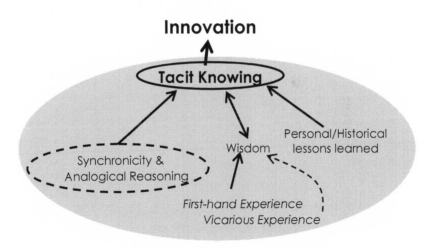

Figure 4: Contributors to Tacit Knowing

Drivers of Innovation

Three sources of innovation have been identified by the renowned management guru, Peter Drucker:

- Incongruity
- Changes in perception, mood, and meaning
- New knowledge

Drucker's sources have specific application to the development of tacit knowledge and synchronicity, which are two of the three central elements for contextual intelligence. Let's look at all three sources of innovation.

Incongruity

Incongruity as a source for innovation requires seeing the world as it actually is, versus the way we presume that it is. And, in a later chapter, we'll discuss several logical fallacies that prevent us from interpreting the world as it really is, since an awareness of these fallacies is an important step in addressing the problem of incongruity. For now, though, we'll describe incongruity as that disconnect between our perception of what is going on and what really *is* going on. We may be able to see incongruity more clearly by recognizing that the opposite of incongruity is congruence, or what may be more familiar to us as agreement. Agreement may be a desirable output, but it is not a necessarily good input (as someone once said, "If we are both thinking the same way, one of us isn't necessary"). The benefit of incongruity comes from wrestling with our differences and learning from the change in perspective that often results.

Our personal blind spots serve as a good example of this. Everyone has a blind spot or two concerning their own behavior and how they are perceived by others. The irony is no one else is blind to it. However, once you are aware of your blind spot, it often helps you interact with the world differently, and this change usually works to your advantage.

How many times have you asked two people who were at the same place, at the same time, doing the same thing about what happened, and got two different stories? This is a perfect example of incongruity. The unique slant of our own perspective often biases what we see. When we begin to see our experiences through the lens of incongruity, we begin to look for non-linear patterns and strange attractors (for descriptions of these terms, refer to Chapter 3). This effort, in turn, leads to new understanding and, ultimately, innovation. Therefore, incongruity is a source of innovation -- though not because you see things differently than others, per se, although you do. It is because you attempt to see the world as it really is (and yourself as you really are).

For example, one of my favorite events is a "blind spot" weekend. Once every couple of years, two of my closest friends and myself find a location away from family and work distractions to undertake what onlookers may see as frivolity. But what is actually going on is rather intense. We put aside the normal rules of engagement and discuss each other's incongruities. We agree ahead of time that there will be no restrictions, and we discuss each other's marriages, each other's parenting, each other's leadership -- you name it. Any incongruity is fair game, and each incongruity, to avoid the possibility of denial, is pointed out with examples by the other two friends. At times, it can hurt, but we believe that the wounds of a friend are faithful. No malice is ever intended and each of us walks away with a deeper friendship and a lot of things to think about. In other words, we are all better informed than when we arrived -- each having a new perspective on our behavior, which often leads to new behaviors.

That said, though, merely recognizing incongruence may not be enough, because realizing that someone is missing the salient factors in a situation, or is drawing inaccurate or incomplete conclusions, is only the first step. The second and most difficult step is being able to articulate the actual reality. But when incongruity is recognized and clearly articulated, the power to create something brand new is almost inevitably generated.

Changes in Perception, Mood, and Meaning

Like the previous source of innovation, being aware of changes in perception, mood, and meaning requires an acute sense of what is happening around you. It requires knowing the what and the why of the changing behaviors and attitudes of others. For instance, people often think they changed their minds based on a logical explanation which makes sense to them. But they failed to recognize what really influenced their decision. Contextual intelligence enables us to be aware of the contributing factors for why others have changed their minds.

Furthermore, those observant enough to see that others' ideas are shifting, and to intervene before they fully shift, are in the best position to lead. I don't mean predicting, guessing about, or forecasting a shift. I mean seeing it while it's happening, when it's still beneath the surface. Being a student of people and human nature, and acutely aware of your own delicate changes in perception, mood, and meaning, is the best place to begin practicing this skill.

For example, do you remember a time when someone close to you had a change of heart, or acted in an uncharacteristic way? Try to remember that time and ask yourself what was going on at a subtle level that prompted that change. Consider what was going on in the background prior to the change. Developing the skills to identify what that background is can facilitate innovation. It does so by making it necessary for you to practice empathy and learn about other people's perspectives.

New Knowledge

The third source of innovation, new knowledge, is not isolated to a single discovery.[22] Although it can be, innovation is not always the result of discovering something brand new – say a new species of animal or something that turns water into fuel. Rather, most innovation that is a result of new knowledge is the meaning that is discovered after assimilating existing knowledge. In other words, it is the meaning that is created from the convergence of several different experiences.

New knowledge often appears, for instance, after a collision between previously unrelated kinds of information. An example is when you realize something for the first time (it may be new only to you, as other people may have known about it for years). But this new realization often ends up producing new behaviors. Another example might be what happens after you make a connection you've never noticed.

Still another example might be how the creation of a team results in new knowledge. Let's say John and Jane have never met before, but they are asked to solve a particular problem together. John brings his personality, experience, tacit knowledge, or the things he knows to be true, but doesn't know why or how he knows, as well as his values to the table. And Jane brings her four qualities, too. Once they begin to interact with a common purpose, their individual attributes begin to mingle and create a third "person," or identity. What arises from John and Jane working together is a new perspective, which facilitates creativity and new experiences for both of them. That is now a reality, and even if John and Jane stopped working together, this new reality will have a ripple effect throughout their organization, reshaping and recalibrating it, as well as both of them, and other stakeholders. Furthermore, it cannot be undone. In the end, this new reality facilitates innovation -- new behaviors, new policies, and new awareness.

To take the concept of new knowledge a little deeper, consider the science of epistemology (the study of how we come to know things) which calls mutually exclusive realities antinomy. The most common example of antinomy comes from theology and is represented by the concepts of free will and predetermination. Both free will and predetermination are theologically true, but one cannot be true if the other is. The concept of mutually exclusive realities, when applied loosely and generically, has particular value for delineating the contextual intelligence model. Contextual intelligence does not accept the notion of irreconcilable differences, and so when two things come together that cannot logically coexist, the only explanation is a new way of thinking -- or the discovery of a new reality.

We hold mutually exclusive ideas all the time, but it only becomes an issue when we are made aware that two or more of our ideas or values are incompatible. Most of us give up trying to reconcile our incompatible beliefs, because it takes too much time, effort, and unlearning. But those who demonstrate high levels of contextual intelligence do not shy away from exploring the irreconcilable differences in their thinking. They are willing to unlearn and relearn, as a function of their contextual intelligence.

The knowledge gained from merging seemingly unrelated (synchronous or vicarious) experiences creates a brand new experience that facilitates a new behavior. Our "incubator" for innovation seems to lie, at least in part, in the ability to connect apparently unrelated contexts, ideas, and people. The notion of new knowledge and a layman's understanding of antinomy provide an important foundation for understanding how synchronicity and analogic reasoning enhance leadership, and create a working model in which contextual intelligence can operate.

Think 360⁰ Exercise 5

Pick an area of your life, it can be either personal or public, and ask yourself when it comes to making decisions within that context what assumptions do you hold to be true without exception, and consider where those assumptions came from.

Which of the drivers of innovation do you most often notice?

Critical Thinking Exercise 5

How much of your decision-making process is based on vicarious experiences?

How might you change those vicarious experiences to first-hand experiences?

PART III

THE 3D THINKING FRAMEWORK

- Introduction to Part III
- 3D Thinking: A Different Orientation to Time
- Leading a Variable-rich Context
- Assembling the Contextual Intelligence Model

Introduction to Part III

Part III will explore time in relation to the practice of contextual intelligence, and will use the following terms for the clarity we can gain from examining the past, the future, and the present:

- Hindsight
- Foresight
- Insight

Figure 5: Hindsight, Foresight, Insight

Hindsight represents those elements of your past which fit a context in your present, bringing new clarity to your decisions and subsequent behavior.

Foresight frames relevant questions about today's decisions that will move you toward a future that brings you closer to a desired image of your future self. (Note that both hindsight and foresight only add value to today; they cannot impact the past or the future.)

Insight is the clarity you experience when aspects of your past are discarded (as being either irrelevant or harmful), so you can see how the past has helped rather than hindered your journey to the present. When combined with the understanding that your desired future should be used to help you move toward it, such insight provides clarity and motivation.

Furthermore, when hindsight and foresight converge, insight is the outcome. And insight, rather than hindsight or foresight, is what you need to leverage in order to make decisions. Insight, meanwhile, requires a healthy and proportionately balanced view of the past and future. Overemphasizing the past, like overemphasizing the future, creates an imbalance that only leads to frustration.

For example, most anxious behavior comes from a disproportionate focus on a past event or future desire. For example, you may exhibit neurotic behavior around snakes, even though the one in front of you is not poisonous, you have never been bitten by one, and you don't know anyone who has ever been bitten by one. But a story from somewhere in your past says you should be scared to death – so you are -- and you allow yourself no rational behavior when it comes to snakes.

An imbalance resulting from overemphasizing the past or future can also manifest in more harmful ways. Take, for instance, the person who refuses to modify his or her spending habits during an economic downturn, using such irrational statements as, "The economy is fine, because as soon as we get a new president, everything will change," or "We Joneses have always had money, so I'm not changing, now."

Remember that there is no such thing as future decision making; all decisions are always made in the present. All feelings are felt in the present. All attitudes are demonstrated in the present. All initiative is taken in the present. And so, this means that decisions, feelings, attitudes, initiatives, and so forth that are taken from the perspective of either the past or future, are neither helpful nor valuable.

Furthermore, having an improper relationship to hindsight can halt your forward momentum. Think of a time when your fear of repeating a mistake prevented you from making a decision. It can be as trivial as not knowing what to order at a restaurant, or as significant as avoiding meaningful relationships.

Likewise, having an improper relationship to foresight can keep you from moving forward. So often, fear that something might not work out the way you hope it will -- or worse, take away something you love, causes stagnation and poor vision. For example, Eastman Kodak invented the digital camera in 1975, but did not invest in the technology for fear it would cut into sales of its film. They were afraid it would herald the death of their most prized product. When digital photography gained popularity in the 1990's, they wanted to enter the digital camera market, but competitors like Fuji and Sony were already a strong presence. So Kodak could never fully capitalize on their invention. By the time Kodak entered the digital camera market in 2001, the company actually lost $60 on each camera that they sold. Nine years later, they ranked sixth in that market, and were on a downward spiral due to smartphones and tablets. Back in 1997, Eastman Kodak shares went for more than $94 a share. But by 2011, their stock had dropped precipitously -- to 65 cents a share. Finally, in December of 2011, the company filed for bankruptcy.

The following chapters will outline how to avoid such short-sighted traps, and offer suggestions for integrating hindsight, foresight, and insight.

CHAPTER 6

3D THINKING: A DIFFERENT ORIENTATION TO TIME

We live in an era where much of the past
cannot be used to describe the future – the
future is so murky that is hard to plan for, and
what matters most is the now.

- Jason Averbrook

Three-dimensional thinking, which is based in hindsight, insight, and foresight, is the rubber that meets the road within the contextual intelligence model (Figure 6). Without a 3D-thinking framework, contextual intelligence has little traction, and is simply a list of leadership behaviors.

Figure 6: 3D Thinking as the Tire

Having the correct orientation to time -- to the past, future, and present -- is a critical success factor in leadership, and a driving force behind performance within organizations.[72] A significant body of literature stresses the importance of time orientation as it relates to the behavior of leaders.[6,8,9,17-19,36,53,72] Scholars have reported 16 popular leadership theories that require some level of awareness of the past, present or future.[72] But the contextual intelligence model requires your simultaneous integration of all three. The simultaneous integration of past, present, and future is what I have come to call 3D thinking and is a hallmark of contextual intelligence.

THREE-DIMENSIONAL THINKING

Within the contextual intelligence model, the past is reframed as an awareness of relevant past events and referred to as hindsight. The future is reframed as an intuitive grasp of the preferred future and referred to as foresight. And the present is reframed as an acute awareness of the present contextual ethos -- all the variables that converge to create a situation -- and referred to as insight (contextual ethos is described in a later chapter in more detail).

Applying the 3D-thinking model of contextual intelligence means that all decisions and actions in the present must be based on hindsight (H) and foresight (F), and can be expressed with the equation:

$$H + F = I$$

In this equation, hindsight and foresight converge synergistically to create insight, and hindsight and foresight contribute equally to the insight needed to inform real-time actions and behaviors. But the value of hindsight and foresight are limited to their contribution to insight. If both hindsight (past, heritage, tradition, or history) and foresight (desired identity, destiny, purpose, or future) are not used simultaneously to add relevant information, then insight is lacking.

Figure 7 is a representation of the relationship between hindsight, foresight, and insight.

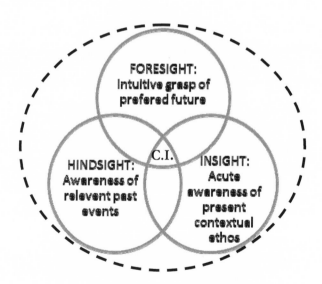

Figure 7: Three-dimensional Aspects of Context

It is the conviction of some scholars that contemporary leadership theories and models are missing the proper treatment of time orientation.[72] Let's look at the utility and meaning of each, in turn:

Hindsight

Previous relationships and experiences influence and even shape present-day behaviors,[72] but the influence of the past is often a passive one. Hindsight involves deliberately recalling experiences and learned lessons (some of which may be completely unrelated to the present situation) that can be applied to the current context. As hindsight is practiced and becomes more developed, it also becomes more intuitive -- though no less deliberate. You've probably heard of "20/20 hindsight," which means it's far easier to understand a complex event in retrospect than when we are living in the middle of it -- but that is not always true (we'll discuss hindsight bias in Chapter 9). Suffice it to say, for now, that hindsight only provides 20/20 vision if you pay attention to where you've been and what you learned while you were there.

Unfortunately, many people misuse hindsight by only remembering bad things. But when hindsight is used correctly, there is rarely room for memories that bring worry or fear.

Foresight

A future orientation represents behaviors that have a direct and purposeful impact on your future, or the future of others, and is what leaders are most measured by. Foresight, furthermore, involves anticipating how decisions and actions can affect the preferred future, and it takes into account unknown and unpredictable patterns. Using foresight in preparing for a hurricane, for instance, would mean stocking up on emergency supplies and preparing an evacuation plan. In a healthcare setting, it might mean creating and rehearsing an emergency action plan with multiple components and several designated leaders. In both cases, it involves doing something today to be better equipped for tomorrow.

In leadership, however, foresight can be less obvious. Ask yourself what you are doing today to make yourself more marketable or a better performer for tomorrow. Even if things are working well right now, you should always be doing something today to put yourself in a better position tomorrow. Let me explain how this mindset works.

We all know that there is some force out there - call it Murphy's Law - that is intent on sabotaging your vacation, but because we are not committed to a routine on vacation, when sabotage strikes we just roll with it. In fact, we may even embrace that unexpected change and have fun with it. On the other hand, when at work and deep into a routine, if the unexpected happens, it tends to derail us. Ironically, it is not the routine that is so troublesome; it is the fact that routine blinds us to foresight. In other words, we don't account for how our present-day actions may impact how we experience tomorrow.

You see, when we are on vacation, we are more mindful of tomorrow because vacation time is finite and we don't want tomorrow's vacation day ruined. So when the unexpected happens, we preempt that possibility by having a good attitude, no matter what happens, and that gives us a new perspective, in turn, on possibilities for tomorrow. This mindset of finite, and therefore valuable, time is what makes leaders tick. Contextually intelligent leaders approach every day as if tomorrow was a vacation day. By doing so, they are always prepping today for a great day tomorrow. This mindset has a profound impact on the application of foresight, because it enables a leader to be proactive towards the unknown.

Insight

A present orientation (insight) involves responding to present-day situations in real time, and is understood to have short-term outcomes. In other words, insight is the convergence of hindsight and foresight in the present moment in a way that informs behavior in real time. Contextual intelligence offers a background for explicit leadership behaviors based on an intentional time-oriented framework (3D thinking).

Here is an example of how 3D thinking can impact your perspective. Most of us believe that the situations we find ourselves in are based solely on the decisions we made in the past. In other words, the problems and challenges as well as the benefits and blessings that you face today are the result of decisions made yesterday. But the notion that the past determined your present is only partially true. Having a proper orientation to time, or thinking in three dimensions, means acknowledging that your present situation is also a component of your hopes for the future, and so is a result of influences from your future as well as your past.

This may seem overly mystical, but I assure you it is not. Consider the often-used saying, "You are more than the sum of your parts." If so, we need to share the credit for the person we are and the situations we are in with more than just our past. This idea aligns with the non-Newtonian concepts of complexity and chaos. In other words, strange attractors are also responsible for the patterns in our lives (described in detail in Chapter 3, a strange attractor is an unknown force that facilitates patterned movements within a chaotic system). Strange attractors pull us into the present, just as our past pushes us there. Following this logic to its natural conclusion, it is necessary to acknowledge that our present situation is just as much a consequence of what we are destined to do in the future, as it is a direct result of our past decisions.

Time-orientation researchers suggest that there are "temporal skills" we can learn which will facilitate an enhanced orientation to time,[72] despite the fact that most of us prefer a single time orientation based on our strengths. For example, we may be biased toward the past (hindsight) because of a long history of success, and so base many of our decisions on what worked in the past. (Note that it is also possible to be biased toward the past due to negative experiences as well; for example, we might refuse to do things because of a negative experience in our past that we haven't yet reconciled.) A preference for a dominant time orientation is called "temporal alignment."[72] But to overcome our bias toward a single time orientation, we must learn to synchronously align all three time orientations at once. The simultaneous alignment of hindsight, foresight, and insight can be facilitated by using the temporal skills of time warping and time chunking. Let's look at the roles these two skills play:

Time Warping

Time warping requires a cognitive manipulation of the past and future by making them seem closer to the present.[72] In essence, it involves using your imagination to skip to some point in the future – effectively "skipping past" the stressful waiting period between the present and the anticipated future. This concept is similar to something theoretical physicists call a wormhole,[79] which is a theoretical compression of space and time that provides a "shortcut" through time. One way to illustrate this in organizational leadership is to realize that it's like helping followers envision the future. Getting others to see a desired end-state helps them make decisions today that move them toward that desired future tomorrow.

This is why such exercises such as writing your own eulogy work so well. But if that idea is too morbid, write a biographical sketch for yourself that captures your achievements two decades from now, when you are about to receive a lifetime achievement award. What do both exercises ask you to do? Use foresight from the perspective of hindsight. In other words, you are using hindsight to describe your future, and foresight to describe your past.

Time Chunking

Time chunking involves grouping together segments (chunks) of time -- for example, referring to segments of time in hours, days, or months. This skill can help you manage future events today, since you can create the future by placing a higher priority on a specific chunk of time (by saying, "We have four weeks to complete this project," you have effectively chunked time together and made that segment more important; that, in turn, reroutes the trajectory of others' efforts so the project is completed on time).

By chunking time together, your overall emphasis becomes the present, a powerful ally of successful leaders. A lot of press time is given to vision statements and strategic planning, and this makes us believe that forecasting the future is where we get the largest ROI (Return on Investment). But I believe this represents a disproportionate orientation to time. Too much emphasis on the future is every bit as dangerous as too much emphasis on the past. In fact, the *only* time orientation that, if over-emphasized, cannot have a negative impact is a time orientation toward the present.

In other words, overemphasizing the past can prove disastrous. Overemphasizing the future can, likewise, prove disastrous. But overemphasizing the present forces you to use contextual intelligence, and if you are going to err, it is far better to err on the side of insight. At least in the present you are not living in an imaginary world, as you would be by focusing on the past and future – both of which are necessarily imagined. And both of which -- if they hinder your appreciation and understanding of the present -- are not being used correctly. Hindsight and foresight can be unwieldy tools if not used with care and discretion. Time chunking is one technique to help you put in proper perspective what you need to do right now to capitalize on the present.

Finally, one exciting aspect of research on time orientation, and the temporal skills of time warping and time chunking, is that such studies imply it is quite possible for leaders to learn 3D thinking.

Think 360⁰ Exercise 6

How will using hindsight, foresight, and insight help you make better decisions?

Which one of the three orientations to time is your biggest distraction, what can you begin to do today to change that?

Critical Thinking Exercise 6

How often does the past hinder you in making decisions and how often does the future cause anxiety? What can you do to integrate 3D Thinking into how you process information?

Chapter Notes and Ideas

CHAPTER 7

LEADING IN A VARIABLE RICH CONTEXT

One day, Alice came to a fork in the road and saw a Cheshire cat in a tree. "Which road do I take?" she asked. Its response was a question. "Where do you want to go?" "I don't know," she answered. "Then," said the cat, "it doesn't matter."

- Lewis Carroll

Educational and cognitive scholars have claimed that intelligence cannot be accurately assessed with scholastic testing or through demonstrated academic prowess.[29,67] Rather, these scholars say, intelligence rests in our capacity for accurately diagnosing and appropriately responding to our environment.

This has profound implications for how many of us perceive the world.

When you investigate the origins of the concept intelligence, you discover that it's a conjunction of two Latin words that can mean to read between the lines – or to decide correctly between multiple options. The notion of reading between the lines is particularly applicable to contextual intelligence. In our contemporary educational system, intelligence has evolved to mean other things, such as the ability to remember and recite information. The culprit for that is our need to measure intelligence – requiring that it be measured has limited our understanding of what intelligence truly is.

But contextual intelligence as a concept involves a re-examination of the wider implications of intelligence and how it is used and measured. I don't believe we will ever stop measuring intelligence explicitly (with grade point averages, aptitude tests, academic achievements), and that is not necessary, but I do believe that our current sense of what intelligence is needs broadening to include behaviors that cannot be explicitly evaluated.

Intelligence as it relates to contextual intelligence is our ability to respond to new situations appropriately, along with our capacity for learning from experience and transitioning between contexts successfully. Robert Sternberg, Yale professor and educational psychologist, has said that any true valuation of intelligence must include contextual indicators. In other words, for us to be truly intelligent, behavior must be considered relative to the specific situation in which we want to exert influence. Ultimately, intelligence is not a trait universally measured in the same way everywhere.[29] And by applying the aforementioned understanding of intelligence, it would no longer need to conform to standardized definitions, but be seen as fluid and dynamic, instead.

In a VUCA world, it is critically important that a leader not only know "how," but also "what" to do, in order to be successful. Knowing *how to* do something is a scholastic-based measure of intelligence and is appropriate when problems are predictable or repeated; knowing *what to* do is a context-based measure of intelligence and is appropriate when problems are unpredictable, novel, or unexpected. Understanding the context in which one operates requires knowing what works within that specific situation, and to know that requires operational knowledge, as opposed to application-based knowledge.[12,34] Application-based knowledge is similar to explicit or declarative knowledge, which is knowledge that can be written down or explained to others. However, operational knowledge requires a keen sense of contextual awareness, which transcends the application of technical skills and techniques.[12]

Ronald Heifetz, founder of the Center for Public Leadership at the John F. Kennedy School of Government at Harvard University, has observed that management is often required when problems are of a technical nature. Solving these types of problems requires the implementation of application-based (explicit) knowledge, by implementing existing policies and procedures. Because these problems are based in a complicated (mechanistic) system, technical problems require little innovation, creativity, or contextual intelligence.

On the other hand, leadership is required when problems have not been experienced before, because leadership is a way of thinking that requires tacit knowledge – which synthesizes solutions from information gained through synchronicity and vicarious experiences, or analogical reasoning. Therefore, intelligence is predicated on recognizing and assimilating experiences and applying tacit knowledge. In other words, leadership potential cannot be fully realized without contextual intelligence.

ADAPTABILITY

Adaptability is the behavioral change required to meet situational demands.[7] It is well accepted that adaptive capacity is one of the most important predictors of performance across a diversity of industries.[15,46,58] Adaptive capacity is certainly a necessary behavior of leaders in contexts that are rapidly changing, uncertain, and complex.[7,82] In contexts where turbulence is continual, leaders must be imaginative and creative, as well as continuously engaged in learning.[74] This means that adaptability (resilience and flexibility) is no longer a mere "coping mechanism" but an imperative.[14,33] That said, adaptive capacity requires a perspective that is different from the one we use to assess our environment and organize information. This new perspective requires an ability to welcome and understand change while it is happening, embrace it as necessary, and modify and adjust our behavior in real time, based upon that change.

As organizations continue to transition from bureaucratic, transactional groups to organic, interconnected teams, the need for us (whether we're in leadership positions or not) to become contextually intelligent increases dramatically. Organizations that continue to evaluate performance based on technical skill, job descriptions, or specialties will suffer.[59] But organizations that evaluate employee or executive performance based on an ability to navigate complexity, uncertainty, and ambiguity, will ultimately prove the most effective and successful.

In turbulent environments, a fundamental element of performance depends upon our ability to monitor subtle shifts in the contextual ethos (the variables influencing attitudes, motives, and behaviors). In ambiguous environments, our awareness of the contextual ethos will help us adapt and respond to those environments. Unfortunately, appropriate adaptation cannot be scripted. So we need to be able to proactively adapt and appropriately respond, something I refer to as improvisational wisdom (described in Chapter 11). If we have a high level of contextual intelligence, we can identify very subtle disruptions in our context, which can be measured by our ability to exert influence in a manner appropriate for the situation.

LEADERSHIP AS A SOCIAL PROCESS

To date, much of leadership development has focused on leader-specific skills, characteristics, and behaviors.[61] This is problematic, in that it creates a distinction between those who have formal organizational roles (manager, executive) and other participants in the leadership process. There are leadership scholars who propose that leadership is actually a social process transcending the skills or abilities of any one person.[11,20,61] In other words, everyone can be a leader. As a social process, leadership focuses on the broader relational and social contexts in which leadership takes place, and must be evaluated in the context in which it occurs. Context, relative to the social process, is understood to be the nature of interactions and interdependencies among and between agents (people, ideas, values, experiences, cultures), political alliances, organizations, religious alignments, social contexts, and private contexts. Contextual intelligence requires an awareness of the interactions between and movement among these agents, as they ultimately inform behavior in a socially complex environment. And while this environment must be considered in light of an unpredictable future, it is still one in which tradition, precedent, and history matter.

Most leadership literature that includes contextual factors confines leadership to the skill needed for a specific job or industry. But it was Frederick Fiedler, an organizational psychologist at the University of Washington, who originally observed that leadership does not take place in a vacuum. This led to later research revealing how the leader and the context reciprocally influence each other.[24,26].

But there is still another missing element: contemporary leadership models need to also include the dynamic nature of contexts, and consider that contexts have dynamic sub-contexts, and that all are influenced by outliers, or yet-to-be-seen variables. In other words, within a given context there is an internal shifting in the variables and the factors that make the context what it is. In addition, there are contexts (sometimes unrelated) that influence other contexts; in fact, contexts are somewhat like planets, in that they can align, collide, or influence each other with their gravitational pull. As a result, it is one thing to learn the specific behaviors, attitudes, and values of a context and thrive within it. But it is something else to transition between contexts across multiple structures. Remember our earlier example of James Scott, while gifted in one context his inability to transition between contexts as a result of failing to understand the values of different groups ultimately led to his downfall.

Another way to explore contextual flexibility is by answering the what, why, when, where, and who questions of stakeholders.[48] Often, the solutions we need are dependent upon a place and time. Context, and not the leader's knowledge or personal background, should define behaviors. Therefore, within the social process, understanding a given context (not the leader's experience, per se) should be the antecedent to action. Failing to consider the context before acting is similar to a physician deciding on a treatment before making a diagnosis.

Keep in mind that taking into account the context does not replace experience, as it is still required for analogical reasoning, but it does facilitate a new perspective. When, for example, you are unexpectedly asked to share the stage at a charity function with the CEO of your biggest competitor and there is a large media presence. In this situation, the rules of engagement change: egos are checked, stage time is not measured, and public relations take a back seat to stakeholder needs. The context dictates that you team up for the sake of your new stakeholders (the beneficiaries of the charity function).

Remember that context is the background of an event. It is the weaving together of several variables that create a web-like pattern of relationships. Therefore, experience becomes a secondary influence in decision-making, while contextual awareness is primary. Like the CEO at the charity function, experience is not ignored; it is instead reframed to provide new meaning.

In a static and predictable marketplace, problems are well defined and formulated; they inherently contain relevant information; have one correct answer; and are unrelated to experiences outside the situation in which the problem manifested. These types of problems are easy to see, evaluate, and solve. Unfortunately, in today's organizational ecosystem, problems are poorly defined; they are missing relevant information; they have multiple possible solutions; and they are influenced by multiple experiences – many of which the problem solvers are not even aware of. Therefore, solving problems and leading in today's organizational climate requires a skill set that transcends what is offered by traditional management techniques and leadership models. In the next chapter, we will present the full contextual intelligence model – which brings everything we have discussed so far together, and adds 12 empirically-based contextual intelligence behaviors.

Think 360^0 Exercise 7

how often do you evaluate performance based
on technical skill and job specific competency
and what would need to occur in order for you
to evaluate performance based on the ability to
navigate complex and in ambiguous situations?

Critical Thinking Exercise 7

How adaptive are you to unexpected change?
What do you think you can do right now to increase your ability to adapt?

Chapter Notes and Ideas

Chapter 8

Assembling The Contextual Intelligence Model

A pilot must of necessity pay attention to the
seasons, the heavens, the stars, the winds
and everything proper to the craft if he is
really to master the ship.

- Plato

When I first used the term, contextual intelligence, almost a decade ago, I intended it to mean a skill set with two parts. The first part is the ability to correctly discern and articulate what is happening in the present moment of time. And the second part is the ability to demonstrate the correct course of action for that moment in time. Since the measures of success change with each situation, demonstrating the correct behavior can be elusive, but contextual intelligence nevertheless involves understanding how to respond correctly to every moment's context.

In my experience, the world is full of people who can discern what is going on around them. That's the easy part. Most people can tell if they are in a hostile or safe, happy or sad environment. What is rare is the ability to know what to do once you know what is going on around you. In other words, many people know they are in a hostile, bad, or even an opportunity-rich situation, but have no idea what to do about it. Of course there are people who misdiagnose their environment and, as a result, routinely make the wrong decision.

If you know people who frequently make bad choices, chances are they are misinterpreting their environment. For these people, learning how to practice contextual intelligence – particularly implementing double-loop learning – can offer a dramatic improvement in their lives. However, it will likely be a long, slow process, as it will mean recalibrating longstanding assumptions and values. It may also be more difficult for them to grasp complexity, tacit knowledge, synchronicity, and 3D thinking. On the other hand, if you know people who are struggling with not knowing what to do, they may be overwhelmed with the complexity and the contextual intelligence model may offer a welcome solution.

In its most basic form, I developed the contextual intelligence model so people would know what to do with the information they had collected about their environment (assuming they have collected useful information). In previous chapters, we discussed the framework in which the contextual intelligence model fits. That framework offered a central axis of rotation (for which we used the analogy of a tire rim) and consisted of complexity, tacit knowledge, and synchronicity. The second part of that framework consisted of 3D thinking, which is the integration and application of hindsight, foresight, and insight.

For this, we used the analogy of a tire, noting that this was not only where the rubber meets the road, it was actually the tire itself. Now, I'll extend that framework to include 12 empirically-based contextual intelligence behaviors (representing the air that fills the tire). When all these elements are integrated, we will have the working contextual intelligence model.

○

Robert Sternberg, an educational psychologist at Yale University, used the term, contextual intelligence, in the early 1980's as a synonym for his concept of practical intelligence, a subtheme within his theory of triarchic intelligence.[67,68] He described it as the ability to apply intelligence practically. Individuals who have a high level of contextual intelligence easily adapt to their surroundings, fit into new surroundings with ease, and can fix their surroundings when they perceive it necessary.

Since Sternberg, contextual intelligence has been used theoretically by different practitioners and researchers in such diverse disciplines as nursing, psychology, business, education, medicine, and politics. And while implicitly similar in meaning, each was heavily nuanced to their specific discipline.[3,12,34,39,52,65,62,70] As a result, the term contextual intelligence – although not new – has been used inconsistently, with very little coherence among the varying definitions and descriptions. In this chapter, we'll look at the operational definition of contextual intelligence while introducing the contextual intelligence model.

As mentioned in previous chapters, context is heavily nuanced. Having the energy to comprehend all the nuances involved in a situation requires the lion's share of intentionality and diligence (Table 2 lists some nuances that contribute to a given context). The integration (sometimes, collision) of these nuances, in part or in whole, is what I have referred to in previous chapters as the contextual ethos. Before we can truly claim to have contextual intelligence, we need to have a grasp of the contextual ethos, and this often requires advance work. Read through the factors in Table 2, and decide how these factors impact all the places in which you want to exert influence. What makes this difficult is that the contextual ethos is constantly shifting and recalibrating, so relying on old or previously gathered information is risky.

TABLE 2: Elements of the Contextual Intelligence Ethos

1. General culture or a society's culture
2. Governance
3. The organization's or context's past (history and philosophical evolution)
4. The paradigms that inform present-day decisions
5. Organizational culture
6. Key players in the organization
7. Political structure and hierarchy
8. Values and attitudes of other stakeholders
9. The decision-making process
10. Perspectives of other stakeholders
11. Idiosyncratic customs
12. Knowledge of how the sociopolitical environment is influencing the current situation

---

As far as I can tell, the first empirical research on contextual intelligence was my own. In 2008, my research laid the foundation for the integration of the concepts of context and intelligence, which later resulted in a conceptual model for contextual intelligence (outlined later in this chapter). The most notable outcome of my investigations proved to be the delineation of 12 behaviors that are directly related to contextual intelligence. This was a huge step toward developing a model of contextual intelligence that was practical, reliable, and applicable. Once the 12 behaviors were identified, it was possible to organize them into a time-orientation framework.

What is most interesting about these 12 behaviors is that the ability to demonstrate them does not necessarily constitute contextual intelligence. They only indicate contextual intelligence when they are practiced in conjunction with each other. This caveat is absolutely essential, because it is the convergence of these behaviors, and not their isolated practice, which signals the presence of contextual intelligence.

For instance, if you demonstrated nine of the 12 behaviors (75%) at a very high level of skill, it would not necessarily mean that you were contextually intelligent. What is required is the integration of all 12 behaviors as a single behavioral cluster, because they are interdependent and do not constitute contextually intelligent behavior by themselves. Therefore, 3D thinking becomes the key for making the 12 contextual intelligence behaviors converge, as it offers a way of seeing the model holistically, instead of as 12 isolated behaviors. Allow me say it this way: Trying to do three things well is easier than trying to do 12 things well. The beauty of this model is that, when you do these three things well (3D thinking), the 12 behaviors become the natural outcome.

Within the framework of our working model, the 12 behaviors are the "air" for the 3D thinking "tire." Without the air, the tire cannot be used for its intended purpose. Below is a representation of the 12 empirically-based contextual intelligence behaviors, serving as the air that fills the contextual intelligence tire.

Figure 8: 12 Behaviors as the Air Filling the CI Tire

The 12 contextual intelligence behaviors have a synergistic effect on each other, and with the addition of 3D thinking, become greater than the sum of their parts.

THE 12 CONTEXTUAL INTELLIGENCE BEHAVIORS

The 12 contextual intelligence behaviors are organized into three groups, according to their 3D category (hindsight, insight, and foresight). Each behavior is briefly described below, followed by questions designed to help you develop or refine that behavior.

Hindsight

Hindsight includes the following four contextual intelligence behaviors: effective use of influence, critical thinker, culturally sensitive, and multicultural leader.

1. EFFECTIVE USE OF INFLUENCE

Appropriately uses different types of power to create a desired influence, or create a desired self-image. Do I know how others perceive me? Am I aware of the actions that create those perceptions?

2. CRITICAL THINKER

Makes connections, integrates, and makes practical application of different actions, opinions, outcomes, and information. How aware am I of my thinking and reactions in real time? Do I self-edit in real time? Am I able to process, connect, and integrate information and practical applications?

3. CULTURALLY SENSITIVE

Works to provide opportunities for diverse members to interact in a nondiscriminatory manner. How inclusive am I of others' ideas? Do I believe that difference equates to richness?

4. MULTICULTURAL LEADER

Can influence the behaviors and attitudes of ethnically diverse people or groups. How well do I understand different cultures and worldviews?

Insight

Insight includes the following four contextual intelligence behaviors: communitarian, mission minded, consensus builder, and diagnoses context.

5. COMMUNITARIAN

Expresses concern about social trends and issues, and participates in civic and community activities. Do I have a sense of social justice? Am I community minded?

6. MISSION MINDED

Communicates how the performance of others affects the mission; aware of how his attitude affects others' perceptions of who he represents. How familiar am I with the mission of my organization? Do I role model the mission and values outside of the organization?

7. CONSENSUS BUILDER

Convinces other people to see the common good, or a different point of view. Which values and goals will win the hearts and minds of others? What outcomes are attractive to others and why?

8. DIAGNOSES CONTEXT

Knows how to appropriately interpret and react to shifts or changes in his surroundings. How aware am I of the contextual ethos? Am I resilient and adaptive to the volatility within change?

Foresight

Foresight includes the following four contextual intelligence behaviors: influencer, change agent, future minded, intentional leader.

9. INFLUENCER

Uses interpersonal skills to non-coercively affect the actions and decisions of others. How do I know that my influence/input has made a difference to the status quo? Write down some examples.

10. CHANGE AGENT

Raises difficult and challenging questions that others may perceive as a threat to the status quo. What are my motives for asking challenging questions? Does my question advance the cause, or does it add roadblocks, instead?

11. FUTURE-MINDED

Has a forward-looking mentality and a sense of where to go in the future; sees beyond present contradictions. What are others doing that is leading edge? What can I learn from them? What are the contradictions in my life?

12. INTENTIONAL LEADERSHIP

Is aware and proactive concerning own strengths and weaknesses, and has delineated goals for achieving personal best and for influencing others. What is my leadership style? Do I know my follower's needs? What are my short-term and long- term outcomes/goals?

DEFINITIONS

Contextual intelligence requires an intuitive grasp of relevant past events, an acute awareness of present contextual variables, and an awareness of the preferred future. The contextually intelligent person is one who appropriately interprets and reacts to changing and volatile surroundings. I have described contextual intelligence in other places using the following description:

> Contextual intelligence is the ability to recognize, assess, and assimilate several external and internal variables inherent in a given environment or circumstance. Simply stated, contextual intelligence is the ability to interpret and appropriately react to changing surroundings... [and] is a skill that separates many leaders from non-leaders... [and] depends on the correct assessment of people.

Critical to this definition of contextual intelligence is the understanding that it also includes an ease of movement between different contexts. But, apart from this definition, there are four obstacles to contextually intelligent behavior (these are discussed in more detail in a later chapter):

- Pace of change
- Failure to embrace complexity
- Learned behavior
- Inappropriate orientation to time.

Learning to overcome these obstacles requires new ways of thinking and engaging with the world – ways that are based on non-Newtonian paradigms, a new time orientation, and the ability to reframe experience. As already pointed out, contextual intelligence is a leadership model that accounts for complexity; requires the use of tacit-based knowledge concepts (analogic reasoning and vicarious experiences); encourages the use of synchronicity; and presents a model that organizes these and other elements according to three dimensions of time. Finally, it includes the integration of 12 simultaneous behaviors, all of which are framed by a deliberate awareness of the contextual ethos. Figure 9, next page, illustrates the entire contextual intelligence model.

Figure 9: Contextual Intelligence Model for Organizational
Leadership

Chapter Notes and Ideas

CHAPTER 9

IMPLEMENTING CONTEXTUAL INTELLIGENCE

Your present circumstances don't determine where you go they merely determine where you start.

-Nido Quebein

It is my belief that contextual intelligence can be acquired,[12] just as I'm convinced that the acquisition of the 12 contextual intelligence behaviors can be learned and even accelerated. Even more exciting is the fact that experience and related constructs (e.g., tacit knowledge and wisdom) can be acquired through such mechanisms as vicarious experience, rather than through more time-consuming firsthand experience. And one simple way to accelerate experience is to continually learn as much about a context as possible. In other words, become familiar with the formal and informal structures in the context you want to influence. This involves knowing who has the power to influence decisions within that context, and how that power is used to control the flow of information.

The contextually intelligent person treats every context as a learning opportunity, and engages in a specific sequence of inquiries in order to learn about each context; what is learned can then be applied in that context as well as other contexts. Furthermore, the experience gained in one context is stored in an "experience bank" that can be called upon at a later time. So no experience, no matter how seemingly insignificant, is ever wasted.

Another strategy that helps facilitate the acquisition of contextual intelligence is learning the language of the target context. But because the term, bilingual, is limited to two languages, I prefer to use the term, co-lingual. Being co-lingual implies that you are able to respond to the structures, processes, patterns, attitudes, values, and influences within any context where you need to acquire or maintain influence.

As a useful analogy, consider how impossible it would be to do business in a foreign country if you didn't know the language,[34] customs, culture, religions, and relevant history. Without a nuanced knowledge of that foreign country, and the intelligence or authority you did have would be useless for gaining the influence required for business.

Becoming Co-Lingual

One of the best ways to become co-lingual is to immerse yourself in new situations. This type of immersion is a tacit-based phenomenon called improvisational wisdom. Immersion only works when the consequences of your actions are immediate, which is the key to gaining new knowledge. Immersion is deliberate, and it entails considerable, specific, and sustained effort. Deciding what you need to learn should be based on what you know you don't do well or can't do at all.[25] If you are delusional enough to believe that you do everything well and that there is nothing you can't do – ask someone else. Immersion is great because it facilitates trial and error learning, which best shortens the contextual intelligence learning curve.

Deliberate immersion should also be preceded by formal study about the context and its relevant and meaningful history (precedent, tradition, and culture). But be forewarned that, if pre-preparation biases you, creating preconceived ideas about that context, it will be detrimental. You must be willing to learn, unlearn, and relearn, at all times. Finally, the acquisition of knowledge about a new context without immersion can be seriously misleading. The reason for this is based on what we talked about earlier concerning incongruity (blind spots). Immersion experiences highlight our incongruities, which when noticed facilitates new ways of thinking (innovation). It is easy to imagine that learning about a foreign country can be significantly enhanced if followed up with a visit to that country. It is likely that what you learned is incomplete or inadequate, which can only be revealed by an immersion experience to that country.

I personally experienced precisely what I am describing. In 2013 I was a Fulbright Scholar to Rwanda where I lived and worked with my family for six months. Before we left for Rwanda we learned as much as we could about the people culture and history. The information that was available to us was heavily concentrated on the 1994 genocide and the HIV epidemic. We arrived in Rwanda with several incongruities, for example we lived in fear of getting HIV and had mental images of people still walking around the streets with machetes. Of course the reality of the situation was completely different. We were pleasantly surprised to find out that Rwanda, and especially their capital city of Kigali – where we lived – was not only civilized, but actually fun and exciting place to live and work. We saw no one walking around with machetes and we never even caused so much as a sniffle. Our incongruity was exposed, which let us all to a new way of thinking, not only about Rwanda but the whole of Africa.

The Contextual Map

Creating a contextual map is another way to acquire the skills of contextual intelligence,[12] and doing so requires three steps:

1. Identifying the factors determining how success is measured in the target context
2. Identifying available resources for predicting obstacles within the target context
3. Creating a framework for comparing performance across multiple contexts

Developing a contextual map using these three steps can yield valuable information, as knowing how success is measured is key to moving forward. Many people mistakenly assume that their idea of success is everyone else's idea of success, but this is rarely the case. In organizational life, finances are usually one of these success metrics, but there are more that need to be discovered. It would be a mistake to assume finances are the only or even the primary metric in every situation. On a personal level, assuming other people have the same measures of success, contentment, or security as you do can also foil your attempts to learn contextual intelligence. Finding out how organizations and people measure success is an important skill to leverage, because once you know how things are measured, you can identify obstacles (identifying obstacles is impossible when success metrics are unknown). Once the success metrics and obstacles are known, furthermore, it is easier to compare performance across multiple contexts.

QUESTIONS CONTEXTUALLY INTELLIGENT PEOPLE ASK

People with contextual intelligence have learned the important skill of knowing how to ask the right questions of the right people at the right time. As a brief aside, though, let's first address the idea of dumb questions. People ask them all the time, and the recipient of such a question will doubtless place a mental note next to the questioner's name about his poor critical thinking ability. So be aware of the questions you ask. Besides, the correct answer to the wrong question may still lead you in the wrong direction.

What are dumb, bad, or wrong questions? Apart from the obvious, they include confrontational questions that challenge the experience, character, or integrity of the person to whom they're directed. Another type of question involves information that is easily looked up; they signal that the question-asker is too lazy to do research. Asking questions like these on a regular basis can seriously threaten your credibility.

That said, asking good questions does not come naturally, but is a skill that requires intentional development. And while it's certainly true that we learn by asking a lot of what we may later realize were "dumb" questions, the trick is to ask them as a novice -- when you will get the benefit of the doubt. Regardless, it's important to learn how to frame and deliver a good question. When you do ask the wrong question, be aware of it and learn from it.

The good questions that people with contextual intelligence tend to ask (examples can be found in Table 3) are usually framed around four general themes:

- Success metrics
- Resources available
- Obstacle identification
- Synchronous benchmarking.

It is important to realize that these questions are not always voiced audibly. Many times, they are asked internally (or reserved for close friends who have no stake in the answer), but asking such internal questions does serve as motivation for finding the answers.

Table 3. Contextually Intelligent Questions

Question Type	(Followed by Sample Questions)

Success Metrics
- Whose responsibility is this?
- How does this influence the anticipated or desired future?
- Who/how is determining what is/is not success?

Resource and Obstacle Identification
- Who has the power and how do they control information?
- Who is supposed to make this decision, vs. who actually makes this decision?
- Who are the recognized leaders?
- Who are the unrecognized leaders?
- Who are the followers and who do they follow?
- What roles need to be accomplished in order for this to get done?

Resource and Obstacle Identification/Synchronous Benchmarking
- What experiences can I relate to this?
- Whose experiences can I relate to this?
- What historical events led to this situation or required decision?

Context is influenced by a diversity of salient factors that create and shape the environment in which we seek to implement and sustain influence and relationships. To achieve influence, asking good questions about our target context is essential.

Contextual intelligence is a leadership model that can be learned and used by any person, in any place, at any time. However, contextual intelligence has specific applications for executives, management-level employees, and organizational leaders, and can enhance our ability to successfully navigate our various environments – including our social, personal, civic, and organizational contexts.

Contextual intelligence is framed around the integration of several factors, including a grasp of complexity (and other non-Newtonian paradigms); synchronicity; double-loop learning; the acquisition and application of tacit-based knowledge; the concept of three-dimensional (3D) thinking (awareness of the past, understanding of the future, acute sense of the present); and the intentional integration of 12 contextual intelligence behaviors. This contextual intelligence framework is best applied in dynamic, uncertain, and ambiguous contexts.

Think 360⁰ Exercise 8

Since contextual intelligence requires integrating all 12 behaviors – and not just demonstrating a high percentage of the 12 – how do you see yourself developing the collective skill set and how long do you think it will take?

Critical Thinking Exercise 8

Which of the 12 contextual intelligence behaviors do you believe is your lowest, why?

What strategies could you implement today to improve that behavior?

Chapter Notes and Ideas

PART IV

OBSTACLES & RECOMMENDATIONS

- Logical Fallacies that Hinder 3D Thinking
- Obstacles and Solutions to Contextual Intelligence
- Recommendations and Action Steps of for Implementing Contextual Intelligence

CHAPTER 10

LOGICAL FALLACIES THAT HINDER 3D THINKING

Finally, whatever is true, whatever is noble, whatever is right… whatever is admirable – if anything is excellent or praiseworthy – think about such things.

-St. Paul the Apostle

The failure to accurately diagnose our current context can lead to mistakes that have a detrimental effect on us and on our organization. Unfortunately, the desire to respond correctly is not enough; the world is full of examples of people who know they need to change, but don't – or, as they are likely to say, can't. Regardless of the reasons, our lack of awareness about the real obstacles preventing an accurate diagnosis is the underlying cause.

114

Most often, the inability to respond correctly is a direct result of our ignorance about the biases inherent in our context, as well as in our own thinking. But this type of ignorance is counterproductive and not at all contextually intelligent. However, as these biases are not always obvious, this chapter will introduce them, since knowing what they are will help you attain higher levels of contextual intelligence. Understanding these biases will also alert you to additional biases that are unique to your contexts, biases that keep you from fully experiencing the benefits of contextual intelligence.

There are two primary sets of obstacles that prevent us from accurately diagnosing our context. The first set consists of logical fallacies, those things that all of us struggle with, and that prevent us from accurately seeing the world and engaging with it effectively. The second, the complexity of context, consists of four obstacles specific to the practice of contextual intelligence (we'll discuss these later), but first let's discuss logical fallacies.

LOGICAL FALLACIES

Failing to diagnose our context correctly is often a result of succumbing to common logical fallacies. While there are many logical fallacies that hinder how we respond to the world, there are three that are particularly counterproductive for 3D thinking, which is an important skill in the practice of contextual intelligence:

1. Hindsight bias
2. Conjunction bias
3. Conformation bias

Hindsight Bias

Hindsight bias is particularly detrimental for 3D thinking because it creates a major obstacle for accurately leveraging the past, since it is the propensity to reinterpret the past in our favor. Most of us have a tendency to rearrange information to support our personal values and beliefs, interpreting events through our unique personal filter – something we are usually unaware of doing. Hindsight bias may manifest, for example, in the oft-repeated statement, "I knew it all along." But what is really happening is, we selectively recall experience that supports the facts we've just learned. And in actuality we didn't know; we were simply emboldened by the recently revealed facts to believe that we did.

Overcoming hindsight bias requires an intentional outlook that includes:
1. Understanding that hindsight bias is always in play
2. Candid conversations with others about what "actually" happened

Each time we fail to recognize how hindsight bias has colored our memory of the past, our contextual intelligence suffers.

Conjunction Bias

Conjunction bias is a bit more difficult to understand, but is perhaps the most detrimental to contextual intelligence. This bias deals with failing to accurately predict the likelihood of an occurrence. We tend to believe something is more probable when there is a lot of information available, simply because we want to use all the information we have. So even if the information is irrelevant, we tend to want to create a use for it. But when we do so, it often leads us in the wrong direction. Box 1, illustrates conjunction bias.

> **BOX 1**
> Linda is 31 years old, single, outspoken, and very bright. She majored in philosophy. As a student, she was deeply concerned with issues of discrimination and social justice, and also participated in anti-nuclear demonstrations.
>
> Which is more probable?
> 1. Linda is a bank teller.
> 2. Linda is a bank teller who attends graduate school at night, and is active in the feminist movement.

Since we want to make use of all the information given, we decide #2 is more probable, when, in fact, #1 is the more probable choice.

Conjunction bias causes us to believe something is more likely because we have information about it. This is particularly problematic because of the enormous amount of often irrelevant information at our fingertips. What is worse is the fact that our need for information can actually become detrimental: when we don't have it, we fabricate it. And fabricating information creates an additional problem called interpersonal mush, a phenomenon described by Gervase Bushe, author of *Clear Leadership*, in which we create stories to explain events we don't understand. For example, a coworker witnesses Joan coming out of the boss's office looking dejected, and leaving the office soon after, even though it's the middle of the morning. He has no idea what is going on, but that evening, while having drinks with coworkers, he tells a story about Joan's termination. He is convinced it is true, and even feels proud for so astutely putting two-and-two together, because he also remembers a water cooler talk – which he saw, but didn't hear – between two of Joan's managers. They must have been talking about her, because the office visit occurred shortly after the water cooler talk. In fact, the managers were talking about a disappointing round of golf earlier that week, and Joan had to leave because her son got in trouble at school for the third time this month.

Imagine everyone's surprise when they see Joan at work the next morning, looking happy and chipper. Now other people are talking about Joan being fired, and a rumor starts. Joan hears about her impending termination, and is now paranoid about meticulously recounting every step she has ever taken. Other coworkers think she is in denial about her termination, wondering why she came in today -- and on and on. (Adding confirmation bias, below, to this scenario, the coworker who started this interpersonal mush is now ignoring Joan's great performance and only looking for her mistakes.)

The solution to conjunction bias and interpersonal mush is to hone your discernment. Discernment, which is too often confused with suspicion, is your ability to judge and perceive accurately. The two best ways to develop greater discernment is to be alert to your biases and frequently ask others – especially those with a perspective that differs from your own – for input. Having discernment will help in determining what information is truly necessary for solving a problem. For what is at stake is, in fact, being able to accurately describe the real problem. We have such a need for gathering information to solve problems that we forget to correctly frame the problem. Honing your discernment can improve your problem-defining skill – which is, at times, a more marketable skill than problem solving.

Confirmation Bias

Confirmation bias is the tendency to seek out, remember, or notice only the information that supports what you already believe to be true. It means having a selective attention span, and it manifests by failing to acknowledge the legitimacy of any information that contradicts your values or ideas. We all want to be right, so we choose what information we consume or believe useful. Unfortunately, when we deem certain information not fit for consumption, it is not only disregarded, it is assaulted (intentionally or inadvertently) with "other" information intended to discredit it. The problem with confirmation bias is that it blinds us to different or novel perspectives – perspectives which can be very valuable.

Take, for example, Jill, a very competent and respected business manager who is asked to prepare a presentation on the new accounting system being implemented at her office. Since she had a hand in bringing the new system on board, she is delighted about the opportunity. While preparing the presentation, she interviews other companies that use it, and is pleased nearly every business manager loved the system for different reasons. Many of those reasons she was not even aware of, and was excited to discover. This new information confirms her belief that the system was the only option for her office.

What Jill failed to realize is that not all the information was positive; in fact, a small handful of business managers did not like the system at all. But she automatically dismissed them because she believed those managers were not using the system correctly, or their "glitches" represented isolated incidents that would not be repeated. Her confirmation bias blinded her from seeing any faults in the new system, and as a result she was inadequately prepared to handle questions from her superiors at the presentation about the system's drawbacks and comparable features between it and their current system.

To overcome confirmation bias, seek out different or even contradictory perspectives and try to understand them. (I am not here advocating compromising or "tolerance" – those are different issues and are beyond the scope of this book.) In spite of a human tendency toward confirmation bias, it is possible to gain a different perspective and engage in effective dialogue with others without violating your core beliefs or values. However, such a dialogue is only productive if you know what your own values are and why you hold them. To engage in this process as a "blank slate" may simply result in frustration.

Think 360⁰ Exercise 9

Which of the logical fallacy identified in this chapter is your biggest obstacle?

Think of times when that logical fallacy hindered you from making the correct decision or seeing something accurately.

Critical Thinking Exercise 9

Develop a strategy where you can identify if a logical fallacy is influencing how you perceive a situation? Let other people know about this strategy.

Chapter Notes and Ideas

CHAPTER 11

OBSTACLES AND SOLUTIONS TO CONTEXTUAL INTELLIGENCE

We exaggerate yesterday, we overestimate
tomorrow, and we underestimate TODAY...
don't underestimate what you can accomplish TODAY!"

-John C. Maxwell

Context means the weaving together of different variables to form an intricate pattern of relationships. Each pattern of relationships is its own context, and is easily influenced by the addition or subtraction of seemingly insignificant or irrelevant variables. Context can also be easily influenced by subtle overlapping or by colliding with another context. As an illustration, think of contexts as coming in various sizes – in micro-contexts and mega-contexts.

Micro-contexts are smaller and sometimes less obvious contexts within larger mega-contexts, while mega-contexts are, of course, large-scale contexts. Micro-contexts often overlap subtly, while mega-contexts often collide. It is important to note that the magnitude of the damage caused by either an overlap or a collision may be disproportionate. Subtle overlaps may have collision-like consequences, and vice versa; this is the nature of chaos and complexity.

Take, for instance, the subtle overlapping that exists between the roles of coworker and friend, the micro-context within the mega-context of work life. While it could be argued that coworker and friend are separate, it is easy to see how these contexts influence each other. There are many examples of subtle overlapping between contexts and the reciprocal relationships or influences between them.

There are also collisions between mega-contexts. But don't mistake collisions for unexpected surprises, as collisions do not occur because no one saw them coming; they occur because of the mistaken belief that mega-contexts can be permanently separated. Many believe, for instance, that our work life and our home life (or any two mega-contexts) can be separated. And those who do believe this find it surprising that, when we are having personal issues at home, it negatively impacts our performance at work. Likewise, when things are going well, either at work or at home, our performance and emotional well-being will be impacted in a positive way. Since the same person is experiencing both work and home life, simultaneously, why should this fact be a surprise?

But many other mega-contexts have the potential for collision. Take, for instance, the continuous improvement of technology, and the never-ending stream of new and relevant information. We know this new information is coming, yet we establish policies, procedures, and behaviors based on old information, and are surprised when the never-ending new collides with our old information. The irony here is that, while we have coping mechanisms for subtle overlaps within a context, it is often the collisions (which we can see coming from a mile away) that we are unprepared for. In part, this may be because shifting variables keep our context in a constant state of flux. Such variables include: political climate, personal values, economic environment, precedent, social and organizational culture, future goals, and stakeholder values – all of which we identified in previous chapters as constituting the contextual ethos.

Adding to the complexity of context is the fact that we may be interacting with more than one context at a time. Staying abreast of constantly shifting contexts requires a unique skill set, one that is actually forcing an accelerated evolution in how leadership and management are practiced. This influences, in turn, how performance is measured and rewarded. Top performers must be able to recognize and diagnose shifts in context as well as know when a new context emerges, and quickly adapt. Failure to adapt, even to the smallest shift, increases the risk of becoming obsolete or irrelevant.

Consider Nancy, the head nurse on the geriatrics floor at a large teaching hospital, who recently found herself in a situation similar to what I just described. Her work station is like the lobby of busy hotel, with phones ringing, monitors beeping, and people constantly coming and going. On this particular day, Nancy is administering medicine to a patient who happens to be the mother of a close friend, although the patient doesn't know Nancy. Before Nancy can leave the room, her friend walks in to visit her mother and introduces Nancy to her mother. The three of them take a few moments to visit and catch up. While this is happening Nancy is aware of a unique dynamic: her personal life and work life have just intersected, and as their visit continues, the lines between the two grow more blurry. Her context has shifted rapidly, as only a moment ago, Nancy's patient was a stranger; in an instant, though, they have become old friends, with a common history. The complexity in this example may have multiple components but is ultimately quite simple.

Nancy's contextual shift from work life to personal life created a brand new set of expectations, and she tries to redraw the new boundary lines by prioritizing the two contexts, placing work first and personal second. But she also notices that her friend is prioritizing their context, making Nancy a friend first and a professional in a medical setting, second. Meanwhile, Nancy feels an obligation to her friend and her mother, but also to every other patient she is responsible for. But even though Nancy's friend is aware of those other duties, she believes they are secondary priorities and holds higher expectations for Nancy (alluding, for instance, to the fact that her mother now has special access to the head nurse).

In the middle of all this contextual sorting, the attending physician walks in with two students and asks Nancy to demonstrate administering an IV tube. Nancy's context and priorities have now shifted again. She has become a teacher being supervised, but is still a friend, with a busy work desk waiting for her. Ironically, all these shifts took place in a five-minute time span, and the only person who is keenly aware of the needed weaving together of all these roles and expectations is Nancy.

○

Unfortunately, leadership has often been seen as a construct that only has meaning to the extent that the context in which it is exerted is understood and defined. In other words, leadership is seen as something practiced relative to the technical competencies required for a specific role. But leadership is now becoming so nuanced and idiosyncratic that it is difficult or even impossible to lead from within a predefined context. And so, instead of isolating context within leadership roles or industries, it is more valuable to teach leaders how to transcend contexts.

For example, if you are an accountant but have aspirations to move into a leadership role, the skills you will be rewarded for will only be those that make you a better accountant. And if you spend your time earning accounting credentials and expertise, that may make you a better accountant, but you will not be seen as a leader.

The S.A.I.D. (Specific Adaptation to Imposed Demand) principle, which states that adaptations are directly related to the stimulus applied, is true for leadership development, as well. For example, if you want to be a virtuoso pianist, you must practice the piano. No amount of playing the violin will ever make you a skilled pianist. It may make you a better musician, but not a better piano player. Likewise, if you want to be a leader, you have to develop leadership skills, not technical or work-related competencies.

OVERCOMING HINDRANCES TO COMPLEXITY

Accurately diagnosing your context is a significant advantage if you can do it effectively, but there are four factors that can hinder you:

1. The pace of change
2. Contextual complexity
3. Learned behavior
4. Incomplete time orientation

The Pace of Change

The fast pace of change can make it nearly impossible to keep up, because once the need for change has been recognized and a solution implemented, it's time to change once more. More specifically, when the rules of the game are continuously altered, or stakeholder expectations are continuously shifting, keeping up becomes increasingly difficult.

One solution, however, is practicing improvisational wisdom, which involves intentionally extracting "life-lessons" from every encounter. In other words, learn as many lessons as possible from as many different situations as possible. Then apply those lessons wherever possible. Remember to not restrict the use of an acquired skill or insight to a single context. Wisdom gained in one context and later applied to a seemingly unrelated context is what improvisational wisdom is all about. An additional benefit of improvisational wisdom is that it may also accelerate the acquisition of experience and facilitate intuitive thinking. So the best way to handle the fast pace of change is to have a rich experience bank to draw from, which will help you with analogical reasoning and the use of synchronicity.

Contextual Complexity

The second hindrance to the practice of contextual intelligence is the complexity of the variables that influence a given context. As global awareness and the need for sustainability and profitability increase, there are ever-growing numbers of external and internal variables that will have an impact on you and your organization. At the same time, they also create a large number of combined variables that create and inform new contexts.

One solution is to embrace the complexity paradox. To do that you must realize that, as complexity increases, the need for having all the pieces in place before a decision can be made, decreases. To illustrate this, consider a simple puzzle with just four pieces. To see the puzzle's picture, all four pieces are needed; a single missing piece will obscure it. But a thousand-piece puzzle that is missing half a dozen pieces is still "readable." And so, as complexity increases, the need to have all the pieces in place before a decision can be reached may not always be necessary.

Learned Behavior

The third hindrance to the practice of contextual intelligence is learned behavior. We are often strongly biased by our existing knowledge and can rarely interpret what we see without bias. And while precedent is useful when an environment is stable, in times of change, precedent is less useful and insight should, in fact, be acquired from additional sources.

One solution is to adopt a new commitment to understanding what informs our behaviors and attitudes, and those of others, our society, and our organization. This requires the continual reframing of experience and is motivationally embedded in improvisational wisdom. The difference is, to reframe an experience, we need to be aware that our existing knowledge may point in the wrong direction, or is influenced by hindsight or confirmation bias, and that the best solution may come from outside our existing frame of reference.

To illustrate how learned behavior can influence how we see and respond to the world, please read the boxed paragraph on the next page:

i cdnuolt blveiee taht I cluod aulaclty uesdnatnrd waht I was rdanieg. The phaonmneal pweor of the hmuan mnid, aoccdrnig to a rscheearch at Cmabrigde Uinervtisy, it dseno't mtaetr in waht oerdr the ltteres in a wrod are, the olny iproamtnt tihng is taht the frsit and lsat ltteer be in the rghit pclae. The rset can be a taotl mses and you can sitll raed it whotuit a pboerlm. Tihs is bcuseae the huamn mnid deos not raed ervey lteter by istlef, but the wrod as a wlohe. Azanmig huh? yaeh and I awlyas tghuhot slpeling was ipmorantt!

You probably had no trouble rearranging the words so they made sense. The ironic part is that you can only read this if you have a lot of experience with the English language. Even more ironic is the fact that this paragraph is literally gibberish, so you rearranged the words to form a reality that fit your experience. In essence, you "lied" to yourself about what the words say – to not appear unintelligent. We do the same thing every day. When we see situations that make no sense, we subconsciously and automatically reorder what we see to fit our experience. Interestingly, after rearranging reality in this way, we then make decisions based on that false reality. This phenomenon is, in some ways, the curse of knowledge.

Reframing your experience requires a close examination of your goals and outcomes. Outcomes are natural byproducts of actions, and goals precede actions. But we have a tendency to make desired outcomes into goals. In other words, what should be a byproduct of intentional behavior becomes, instead, the goal. Every time this occurs, the environment must be artificially manipulated in order for that reversal to happen. The solution to this is being sure that the desired outcome is not the goal we focus our efforts on.

For example, many people talk about communication being a problem, and make "improving communication" a goal. That sounds noble, except for the fact that communication is actually an outcome. If you make it a goal, you have to insert something artificial into the context for it to occur, and if it does occur, it is unnatural. Therefore, when reframing your experience, check whether your goals should be outcomes, instead. Getting them in the correct order will lead to a reevaluation of your actions and put you closer to your desired outcomes (which are, by the way, better than accomplishing goals). In short, focus less on accomplishing goals, and more on demonstrating behaviors that lead to your desired outcomes (unlike the misguided accountant mentioned earlier). At the very least, be sure to have goals and outcomes in their proper place, or order.

Incomplete Time Orientation

The last hindrance to the practice of contextual intelligence is a disproportionate time orientation. Most of us, when faced with a crisis, a shift in context, or an important decision, lean heavily toward one of three time orientations -- the past, future, or present. We disproportionately apply information from one of these orientations, rarely consulting all three simultaneously or proportionately. This can prove unproductive, especially if the wrong time orientation is consulted.

The solution to this is to think in three dimensions; 3D thinking requires an awareness of how the past, future, and present influence the current context, and is the application of hindsight, foresight, and insight. Implicit to thinking in 3D is knowing whether it is appropriate, and when to emphasize one time orientation over another (for more on 3D thinking, see Chapter 3).

ACQUIRING THE CONTEXTUAL INTELLIGENCE
BEHAVIORS

Once the four solutions to these hindrances are put in place, we can use them to develop, organize, and integrate the 12 contextual intelligence behaviors, as contextual intelligence necessitates weaving these behaviors together. This is a heavily nuanced ability, in the sense that each of these behaviors must be practiced in conjunction with all the others, or simultaneously. Practiced alone, a single behavior may contribute to leadership skills, in general, but when these behaviors are practiced together, that is what will lead to contextual intelligence. Descriptions of the 12 contextual intelligence behaviors are listed in Chapter 8, and the following section provides brief suggestions for acquiring or developing each of the 12 behaviors.

INFLUENCER

Look for opportunities to practice your interpersonal skills and to exercise different types of power. Here are five types of power you can exercise:

Legitimate: Similar to the concept of jurisdiction, this comes from the belief that a person has the right to make demands and expect compliance

Reward: This results from the ability to compensate another for compliance

Expert: This is based on a person's superior skill and knowledge

Personal or **Referent:** This is the result of a person's perceived attractiveness, worthiness, and right to respect from others

Coercive: This comes from the belief that a person can punish others for noncompliance

Contextual intelligence requires using different types of power judiciously and preferentially. For example, you should strive, first, to use power primarily from the personal or referent category. If that does not work, expert power can be tried, followed by legitimate power. Reward power should be used last, and coercive power should be avoided. (Note that the rules for coercive power may change as context changes; one example might be in a military setting where coercive power could be appropriate.)

To use these types of power, practice creating and sustaining influence without reward, coercion, or manipulation. To do that, help people see how advantageous an idea or a change is to them, while not drawing attention to how it benefits others or yourself. Start with small goals in order to increase your confidence.

CHANGE AGENT

Do not be afraid to raise issues that challenge the status quo, but don't always play the devil's advocate, either, as that can become annoying and people will discount your credibility as an objective thinker. A change agent must have a sound rationale for wanting to challenge the status quo, so be sure to become skilled at articulating your rationale. When initiating change, pick low-hanging fruit first, to gain confidence as a change agent. And work to gain legitimate credibility and trust with those around you.

FUTURE-MINDED

Read widely from an international perspective. Dream of possibilities and potential developments, always keeping your eye on the horizon. Be sure to articulate a coherent picture of the future

– by describing how current and future obstacles to attaining the desired state can be overcome. Develop an intentional network, one that is international in scope.

INTENTIONAL LEADERSHIP

When forming a leadership team, make sure you select people who complement your weaknesses, and are not afraid to talk to you about them. Also enlist the help of others who have a different or unbiased perspective. Typically, these helpers come from outside the context in which you intend to demonstrate intentional leadership.

EFFECTIVE USE OF INFLUENCE

Consider critical feedback a gift. Actively seek criticism from others, especially those with whom you share values, but have different ideas. Begin to learn about the people around you who look to you for advice or direction, and know when and how to appropriately interact with them in different settings. For example, you may have to use reward power with a specific employee today, but you may need to exert legitimate power with that same person tomorrow.

CRITICAL THINKER

Build relationships with colleagues that transcend the workplace. Ask for feedback to discover what was intended, relative to what actually happened. Be able and willing to unlearn, and relearn, what you think you already know. Ask trusted colleagues to help you critically appraise your behavior in real time.

CULTURALLY SENSITIVE

Look at who you interact with at work, or in your community. Be interested in their experience and background. Seek out friends and advisors with experience and backgrounds that differ from your own. Show genuine interest in learning about the histories of people outside your normal circle of friends.

MULTICULTURAL LEADER

Study a variety of world cultures and religions, and when leading or forming teams, strive to include cultures and worldviews that differ from your own. Promote recruiting efforts that identify multi-cultural candidates. Make multi-cultural experiences an explicit part of your own career development and the career development of followers.

COMMUNITARIAN

Become involved in a community, or in civic outreach, and ask friends and colleagues to join you. At first glance, this may seem to be the least related behavior to your job or industry, but as a community and global citizen, it is a hallmark of contextual intelligence. Be able to articulate how local and federal laws and regulations impact how you and your coworkers can accomplish your job. Read widely to keep up to date on geopolitical and socioeconomic developments.

MISSION-MINDED

Be aware that your behavior always reflects positively or negatively on the people and groups you represent. Look for mentors from within your organization who exhibit the company's values in the local community. In other words, identify colleagues who model valued behaviors, regardless of the setting they are in.

Identify what makes them stand out, and practice their best qualities until those qualities become second nature to you.

CONSENSUS BUILDER

Practice painting the big picture in such a way that others become enthused, want to contribute, and are eager to participate. Realize that consensus does not mean unanimity. When debating or dialoging about a new idea be sure to lay out all the ground rules beforehand, but once the ground rules are clearly delineated, facilitate discussion rather than expressing your own opinion too vehemently. The consensus builder's will is best realized by delineating the ground rules for discussion. Once the discussion is complete, be sure to summarize what was decided and why.

DIAGNOSES CONTEXT

With a colleague or friend, routinely evaluate your interpretation of your context and all the contributing factors of its contextual ethos.

●

Integrating these 12 behaviors is fundamental to the practice of contextual intelligence. Demonstrating these 12 behaviors, in conjunction with overcoming the four hindrances to the ability to handle change and lead across multiple contexts, can lead to a competitive advantage. In other words, developing contextual intelligence is conducive to becoming a top performer with fewer boundaries, one who is able to maintain influence across multiple contexts.

Think 360⁰ Exercise 10

Which of the four obstacles – pace of change, level of complexity, learned behavior, or inappropriate orientation to time – is your biggest deterrent to performing at a higher level?

How can you begin to implement the recommended solution to that obstacle today?

Critical Thinking Exercise 10

Which of the strategies for the development of the 12 contextual intelligence behaviors would be the easiest for you to start, why?

Chapter Notes and Ideas

CHAPTER 12

RECOMMENDATIONS AND ACTION STEPS FOR IMPLEMENTING CONTEXTUAL INTELLIGENCE

The gentile reader will never, never know
what a consummate ass he can become,
until he goes abroad.

- Mark Twain

How can contextual intelligence be integrated into your day-to-day life and behaviors? You may understand the tire analogy, but what can you do, right now, to improve your contextual intelligence?

Before offering recommendations, here is one caveat. Earlier, we discussed non-Newtonian principles (complexity and chaos) as a component of the contextual intelligence tire rim. As part of this rim we must embrace the fact that implementing contextual intelligence occurs in a complex environment. In other words, integrating it is not as simple as outlining sequential steps. In fact, having a 1, 2, 3 approach to cultivating contextual intelligence contradicts the framework itself.

Delineating sequential steps can be helpful, but before any steps can actually make a difference, you first need to grapple with the notions of complexity, tacit knowledge, and synchronicity. In so doing, pay special attention to how those concepts and ideas manifest in the day-to-day operation of all the different contexts in which you find yourself. If necessary, re-read Chapter 11 and discover how the four obstacles to contextual intelligence and 3D thinking are present in your situation; then apply the recommended solutions.

It may be that all four obstacles are not present for you, or that only two of four, or one of four are issues. Go back and review the solutions in the previous chapter, which are more conceptual than the forthcoming action steps, and begin to adjust and recalibrate the way you think about all the contexts in which you wish to have greater influence and authority.

This is no easy task. It's something that cannot be accomplished overnight. In my experience, it takes varying amounts of time to disassemble mental models that have taken years and even decades to construct. Most likely, it will also require the help of others. We all have an amazing capacity to not see in ourselves what is painfully obvious to everyone else. And so, applying the recommended solutions of practicing improvisational wisdom, embracing the complexity paradox, reframing our experiences, and thinking in 3D is a massive undertaking that will require the help of others. The only way to make contextual intelligence a tacit behavior is to weigh the outcomes of your actions and consider the consequences of behaviors. For this to take form in a way that can actually help you become a better leader, you must make your intentions known to others.

For example, if reframing experiences is a strategy that you wish to use, do not do it alone. Make the decision to do this publicly and then allow other people to help you. The same advice applies to all the recommended solutions, whether you intend to implement one or all four. Once you have committed to understanding the issues at the tire's rim (after enlisting others' help in remaining accountable, while applying the general recommendations), then the following 14 action steps for acquiring greater contextual intelligence will have more impact.

ACTIONS STEPS TO IMPLEMENTING THE CONTEXTUAL INTELLIGENCE BEHAVIORS

ACTION STEP 1

Develop a Contextual Intelligence Action Plan

Many resources are available to guide you through this first action step. The best place to begin is by completing the online Contextual Intelligence Profile™ (CIP™) at **CIprofile.com**. The CIP™ measures your contextual intelligence on four levels. First, it measures how well you are simultaneously integrating the 12 contextual intelligence behaviors. Second, it measures how you are demonstrating each of the 12 behaviors. Third and fourth, it provides an overview (both symmetry and magnitude) of your 3D thinking. Once you complete the CIP™, use the results to identify specific behaviors that need improvement or to locate 3D thinking areas that require greater attention. You can also make use of the *Contextual Intelligence Implementation Work-*

book, which walks you through several sequential steps and activities intended to develop a customized actionable plan for increasing your contextual intelligence, and is available in the appendix of this book, or on line at CIProfile.com.

ACTION STEP 2

Perfect Your Ability to Extract Lessons and Knowledge from Every Experience

Enlist the help of others, especially those familiar with your past, to accurately remember what has occurred in your life, and how those experiences influence your behavior and decision making. This exercise should also help you be able to examine the value of current experiences. For example, try to find solutions to problems in one context by using experience from other contexts. This forces you to see the value of all your experience, and facilitates "out of the box" problem solving.

ACTION STEP 3

Transform Knowledge into Wisdom that Can Be Reused in New Contexts

Try to uncover the tacit background behind what you believe to be true. You can do that by identifying what you believe about life, and exploring why you believe things happen as they do. Examine why you believe something is true. Is it because it actually is (you have seen it happen)? Or is it because of some other reason? In other words, are you establishing a core value or belief on a rock-solid foundation, or on an untested observation? After you determine what is authentically true, then its truth should transcend context and be true everywhere, all the time. Use that confirmed knowledge as a resource for providing solutions to problems in all the contexts (micro and mega) in your life. This action step will require vigilant discipline and honesty, as well as input from others. But remember that wisdom is something that can be built upon, and the quality and longevity of a solution is only as good as the wisdom used to create it.

ACTION STEP 4

Act Quickly When the Circumstances and Events Surrounding Your Context Change

Reactivity as a response to changing circumstances is based on instinct, and instinct is a poor substitute for reflexivity, the best response in such circumstances. Another common response, presumption, is, as you already know, always a bad idea. The best course of action is to train your reflexes and not your instincts, and the difference between instinct and reflex is more than semantics.

Instinct is based in a Darwinian presumption that all behaviors are self-serving and cannot be helped. Reflex, on the other hand, is a physiological phenomenon based on neurological patterns developed through repetition. When we rely on instinct, we can be led astray -- and even develop a false sense of what is true and natural -- while tending to become over-reactive. But when we train and develop our reflexes (much the way athletes do, with such techniques as plyometrics and Proprioceptive Neuromuscular Facilitation), we can trust our responses. The way to train our reflexes, in an organizational or leadership context, is to practice making decisions quickly, by using hindsight, insight, and foresight. This may sound like lunacy, and it may indeed be, so start with smaller decisions.

ACTION STEP 5

Leverage All Five Senses

Have you ever tried to describe the color red to someone who cannot see? Obviously, the color red needs to be experienced firsthand in order to be appreciated. Relative to leadership, everyone has the capacity to use all five of their senses. The five senses help us understand and relate to our surroundings. Far too often, though, we only use one or two senses. But when we do engage all five, the richness we gain while interacting with our surroundings increases dramatically. Here is how the five senses and their organizational counterparts can be applied to decision making:

1. Sight is equivalent to vision and foresight
2. Smell is equivalent to hindsight and path finding
3. Touch is equivalent to insight, awareness of the present and proximity
4. Taste helps us distinguish between flavors (sweet, sour, bitter) and is equivalent to discernment
5. Hearing is equivalent to active listening

In our physical world, all five senses instantly contribute information about our surroundings. In organizational decision making, it works in much the same way. Foresight, hindsight, and insight converge to give a three-dimensional picture of the past, present, and future. Hearing helps us understand the values of the stakeholders, and taste lets us know about the organizational climate -- if the people involved are adversaries, allies, bedfellows, or opponents (see Action Step 9 for a description of these four categories).

ACTION STEP 6

Balance All Feedback

Input means all the perceived information that influences a situation. In the field of exercise physiology, scientists know your body reacts to both feedback loops and feed-forward loops. Most of us take advantage of feedback, say, when reviewing a performance evaluation or 360° assessment. But feed-forward involves preparatory adjustments to obstacles in our path as we encounter them. For example, elite runners will often make slight adjustments in their running stride and cadence when they notice obstacles – sticks, rocks, potholes – on their running surface, without altering their pace, speed, or forward momentum. Feed-forward can be defined as those automatic adjustments that occur in real time (see action step 4) when obstacles are identified, and there is no time to stop and create an alternate course of action. Both feedback and feed-forward are inputs that should be used by organizations and by leaders.

Another form of feedback that can be applied to contextual intelligence is teleoanticipation, which means to achieve an expected end. Currently, it is a term used exclusively within the track and field community for a subconscious pacing mechanism that runners use to ensure that their maximum effort is always in play. It is the brain's subconscious monitoring of the body's responses to internal and external stresses. The brain subconsciously monitors a variety of different inputs, and tells the runner when he is ready to give another maximum effort in a series of such efforts (intervals). In other words, it is an internal regulatory mechanism enabling a runner to exert maximum effort as often as possible. It allows for rest and recovery, but never too much rest or too little recovery.

When teleoanticipation is compared to other metrics of readiness (heart rate, blood pressure, respiration rate, rest time), training can occur at higher intensities or, as a result, in less time. In other words, athletes who rely on teleoanticipation, instead of other external markers of readiness, demonstrate higher efficiency.

Leaders can improve their use of input by finding out what constitutes success for each situation they are in. Having an awareness of how you determine success versus how others determine success – and responding to any difference between the two – is one way you can apply feed-forward and teleoanticipation in the practice of leadership.

That said, the application of teleoanticipation to contextual intelligence, and ultimately leadership, is profound. You can learn teleoanticipation by balancing all of the feedback from steps 4, 5, and 6, and, as a result, learn how to give maximum effort with minimum fatigue.

ACTION STEP 7

Look for Non-Linear Patterns

Chaos and complexity are here to stay, but do not make the costly mistake of confusing chaos with disorder. Chaos is orderly and patterned, but it is not linear. However, sequential (linear and mechanistic) patterns no longer exhibit the predictability they once did. So learning to identify non-linear patterns, by including outliers in your calculations, is critical in today's marketplace.

ACTION STEP 8

Anticipate that Outliers Will Influence Outcomes

In the realm of complexity, outliers are more significant than we might initially believe. Outliers are observations that deviate significantly from what is considered normal or predictable. And while outliers are unexpected, they are not unnoticed. A word of caution, do not confuse anticipating outliers in decision-making with failing to eliminate irrelevant information. It is a common practice to ignore or exclude information that is irrelevant to a problem, and this is a tried-and-true tactic that can serve you well. However, do not be too eager to assume that outliers are irrelevant. In a linear or Newtonian-based system, excluding outliers is an acceptable practice for drawing inferences. But as we now live and make decisions in a VUCA (volatile, uncertain, complex, and ambiguous) world, discounting outliers could be detrimental. Ultimately, this action step is about perceiving the interactions between objects that are distant from one another, and the consequences of those interactions.

For example, don't underestimate the domino effect that one relatively minor decision can have. When going through the consequences of a decision, never follow through on it if your response to one of them is, "That will never happen." In other words, have a plan for consequences that will never happen.

ACTION STEP 9

Know Whom to Ask for Insight When You Have No Experience to Draw From

After you have exhausted your internal experience bank (vicarious and firsthand experience), who is your go-to person when you need advice about something that you have no prior experience, no "grid" for? Once you have identified that person, ask where he or she fits within what Peter Block, author of *The Empowered Manager*, calls an Agreement-Trust Matrix. To determine that, ask yourself these two questions:

1. How much do I *trust* this person?
2. How much do I *agree* with this person?

Your answers will determine which category your advisor fits into, relative to the agreement-trust matrix (Table 4). For example, someone with whom you have a high level of trust and a low level of agreement falls into the opponent box, while someone with whom you have a low level of trust and a high level of agreement falls into the bedfellow box.

Table 4: Agreement-Trust Matrix

	Low Level of Trust	High Level of Trust
High level of Agreement	Bedfellows	Allies
Low level of Agreement	Adversaries	Opponents

Depending on the problem you need to solve, people in each of the four categories offer both pros and cons. The lesson is not to discount anyone, but to be cognizant of where people fall within the matrix. It is also possible for a single person to fall within multiple boxes, depending on the problem or issue. For example, when creating a new performance evaluation for subordinates, your supervisor could be an ally. But when determining who the best person to be the new plant manager is, he maybe an opponent. Most often, though not always, the best person to ask for insight is an opponent, because he or she offers a different perspective but has your best interests in mind.

To take this action step one step further, you need to know why people are attracted to you. Generally, people become your friend for one of three reasons:

1. They love what you love
2. They hate what you hate
3. They are attracted to you regardless of your likes and dislikes.

It is important to assess why the people around you are there. Many associates and friends hang around as long as there is something you mutually love or hate. Once those things are gone, the relationship usually changes. It can also be a metric for the motives of those who are around you. Use this same metric to determine why *you* are attracted to certain people. Do you love what they love, hate what they hate, or just genuinely like him or her as a person? Most of our friendships are based on mutual "likes," secondarily on mutual "dislikes," and thirdly, on a genuine attraction.

ACTION STEP 10

Explore the Nuances within Situations and Contexts

While this step may appear similar to Action Step 8, including outliers, it extends that step by taking into account subtle differences in meaning. The term nuance is of French origin and represents mists that ever-so-slightly obscure the true color of an object. It is, in essence, the not-so-obvious variance intrinsic within contexts. The best way to calculate for nuance is by asking informed questions of all stakeholders, and especially, of outliers, opponents, and adversaries. But focus groups for a target audience won't help with this action step. When done well (good questions asked of the right people), it allows you to see the different meanings people project onto a context. Another aspect of this step requires being aware of which mist is shading your own vision (often you will need help from others to see this accurately). This action step takes time and pre-work. Eventually, you will become better at doing it intuitively; but initially, it requires intention, input from others, and patience.

ACTION STEP 11

Learn to Manipulate the Future with Appropriate Actions in the Present

Many of us have a propensity for overestimating the value of the past and future, while underestimating the value and significance of the present. But the present is the only acceptable time to demonstrate desired behaviors. The past is literally a figment of our imagination, and is only valuable to the extent that it helps us understand the present. Anything from the past that does not add value to our present should be put aside. Likewise, the future is also imagined, and its only value is in motivating us to demonstrate a desirable behavior in the present. Manipulating the future correctly can only happen if we focus more on right now than we do on tomorrow (focusing on the future is actually a deterrent, if you wish to encourage actionable behavior). So if you want something to happen tomorrow that is different from today, do something different today.

ACTION STEP 12

Recalibrate Goals and Outcomes

Earlier on we discussed the problem of replacing outcomes with goals. This action step is an intentional reminder to be vigilant about critically analyzing your goals, and not allowing outcomes to become goals. Stated simply, this action step requires you to consider all goals as outcomes. To do that, create a list of goals and objectives on paper, and then rename your list "outcomes." Now that you have a list of intended outcomes, work backwards by asking what behaviors are necessary for these outcomes to be realized.

ACTION STEP 13

Become Literate in Framing the Problems of Different Disciplines

Contextual intelligence involves being mindful of how a context impacts others. To do this well, you need a well-developed sense of empathy. And developing this degree of empathy necessitates learning about the values, history, motives, and morals of others – including those of competitive organizations, or completely unrelated disciplines. The danger here (the counterfeit skill set) is to speculate about what stakeholders want, but don't do that. Instead, try to understand and articulate the problem from another perspective. To start developing this skill, pick an organization, person, or industry (one that you are not too familiar with, don't often agree with, or one that you do not care that much about) and learn enough to intelligently analyze how change (federal regulations, local politics, the economy) would impact them. In other words, force yourself to see things from other perspectives, and put into words what they themselves might be proud to say. One word of caution: Be vigilant not to lose yourself, or your own values and convictions, during this process, but do the process, nonetheless.

ACTION STEP 14

Learn to Be Retroflexive

Retroflexion is a powerful concept that describes a change of position without a change in location. You are retroflexive if you are agile enough to turn 180 degrees (essentially, to face in a completely new direction) without losing your sense of where you are. In other words, you can seriously entertain new ideas without compromising your values. As a retroflexive person, you can see many sides of an issue without losing your sense of what the issue is about.

Many people get confused and frustrated when asked to think about something from a different perspective, because they forget what they themselves were thinking. Learning to be retroflexive is as easy as being sure of what you think about an issue, topic, or idea before you start entertaining others' ideas on the issue. One way to develop this skill is to write down what you think and why. Once that is articulated, begin to develop arguments for and against the idea that you just adopted. Learning to be retroflexive provides a perfect balance between becoming so open-minded that you have no convictions, and being so stubborn that you are dogmatic and fail see any other perspective.

●

By implementing these 14 actions steps, you can make significant strides toward greater contextual intelligence. As an interesting aside, by implementing these 14 steps *without* integrating the contextual intelligence model and the 3D thinking framework, you may be able to make others believe that you are more contextually intelligent than you actually are.

That said, legitimate contextual intelligence centers on having a keen grasp of the complexity and chaotic nature of each of the contexts in which you find yourself. It requires a purposeful application of synchronicity and an intuitive awareness of your own tacit knowledge. It's a good idea to learn to appreciate how these concepts influence you and others, though learning this is not an academic pursuit, and neither is this "classroom" a conventional one. But make no mistake, the pursuit of this form of intelligence is rigorous and the course of study intense. The proof of acquired knowledge is in changed behavior, and that can be very rewarding.

Developing the 12 empirically-based contextual intelligence behaviors within the framework of 3D thinking is, likewise, a rewarding endeavor. Appropriately using hindsight, foresight, and insight requires intentionality. But it can save your sanity and give you extremely valuable perceptions and perspectives. As an "intelligence," it is necessary to understand that learning it quickly should not be the goal. Contextual intelligence is an outcome that has to be preceded by understanding the central framework, endeavoring to think in 3D, and being vigilant about developing all 12 contextual intelligence behaviors, equally.

Think 360⁰ Exercise 11

Of the 14 action steps, which one can you start tomorrow? How will you do it?

How long do you think it will take for you to be significantly more contextually intelligent, what is most likely to facilitate that development, and what is most likely to hinder that development?

Critical Thinking Exercise 11

Which action step is the most difficult for you to understand? What can you do to learn more about that action step?

Chapter Notes and Ideas

Glossary

3D Thinking = the integration and convergence of hindsight, insight, and foresight.

Adversary = an individual with whom you have a low level of trust in a low level of agreement.

Ally = an individual with whom you have a high level of trust and a high level of agreement

Ambiguity – where the causes and the "who, what, where, when, how, and why" behind the things that are happening are unclear and hard to ascertain.

Analogical reasoning = using a similar experience instead of a direct experience to draw inferences about your situation.

Antinomy = two mutually exclusive truths.

Bedfellow = an individual with whom you have a low level of trust and a high level of agreement.

Chaos = a system of thinking where you believe things can be non-linear and still patterned.

Co-lingual = the ability to understand more than one context or culture

Complexity = an open system where outliers and external variables may have a significant influence on outcomes and behaviors; and where solution and answers can be found within or outside of the established system. Numerous difficult-to-understand causes and mitigating factors involved in a problem.

Complicated = a closed system where outliers do not matter and solutions and answers are found within the established system.

Confirmation bias = a kind of logical fallacy where people ignore information that contradicts their belief and only accept information that confirms their belief.

Conjunction bias = a kind of logical fallacy that places a disproportionate value on available information, and leads to a faulty assumption of probability.

Context = the weaving together of the background events that constitute a situation or attitude.

Contextual ethos = the complex mix of several different variables.

Contextual Intelligence = the ability to quickly and intuitively recognize and diagnose the dynamic contextual variables inherent in an event or circumstance that results in the intentional adjustment of behavior in order to exert influence appropriate for that context.

Double-loop learning = an internal assessment based on how well one is performing relative to the environment in which they are in and a real time adjustment of their behavior when needed.

Epistemology = the science of how we come to know that something is true.

Explicit knowledge = knowledge that can be transferred through formal means, such as reading and writing.

Feedback = type of reflexive input that is based on previous information.

Feed-forward = a type of reflexive input that is preparatory based on anticipation.

Firsthand experience = direct experience of an individual.

Foresight = an anticipatory function based on the awareness of the preferred future that informs present day decisions.

Goals = actionable behaviors that one intends to demonstrate

Hindsight = a function of memory that provides information to present-day decision-making based on relevant past events.

Hindsight bias = a logical fallacy whereby an individual remembers their involvement in a situation in a more positive light than what actually occurred.

Improvisational wisdom = he wise action that is based on vicarious experience

Incongruity = the disconnect between what has truly occurred and your perception of it.

Innovation = and idea, service, or product that is brand-new or never before seen.

Insight = the convergence of foresight and hindsight that gives relevant information for decisions that need to be made now.

Intelligence = the ability to read between the lines and choose between two viable options that result in the appropriate response in any given situation.

Logical fallacy = faulty beliefs that lead people to believe they are smarter or more accurate than they really are.

Macro-context = the large-scale context in which we live and navigate. Examples = work, family, politics, religion, etc.

Micro-contexts = the smaller sub- or meta-contexts (i.e., roles) within the macro-contexts of our lives. Examples = typical roles of the man within family context are father, husband, provider, disciplinarian, handyman, lover, etc.

Non-Newtonian thinking = appreciation of the world and how it works from a non-mechanistic or linear vantage point, e.g., quantum mechanics.

Nuance = the slight variances observed in different situations, people, and events.

Opponent = an individual with which you have a high level of trust and low level of agreement.

Outcomes = the result or natural byproduct of an action.

Phase transition = the unstable or unknown state that lies between two known states.

Retroflexion = a change of position that does not require a change of location.

ROI = return on investment

Strange attractors = an unseen force that facilitates patterned movement in chaotic systems.

Synchronicity = meaningful coincidence or two or more unrelated experiences converging in a moment in a meaningful way.

Tacit knowledge = things that you know to be true, but are unsure of how or when you came to know them; and are therefore difficult to teach to others.

Teleoanticipation = a subconscious mechanism whereby the brain supplies information to the body about the amount of effort is able to exert.

Time chunking = grouping together large segments of time.

Time orientation = one's natural disposition to favor the past, the present, or the future in decision-making.

Time warping = the skipping past segments of time to a preferred end state.

Uncertainty – where major "disruptive" changes occur frequently. In this environment, the past is not an accurate predictor of the future, and identifying and preparing for "what will come next" is extremely difficult.

Vicarious experience = embracing and adopting the experiences of someone else as your own.

Volatility – where things change fast but not in a predictable trend or repeatable pattern.

VUCA = volatile, uncertain, complex, and ambiguous.

Worm hole = a theoretical compression of space and time.

TABLE OF CI BEHAVIORS (CONT. NEXT PAGE)

BEHAVIOR	DESCRIPTION	KEY QUESTIONS	HOW TO ACQUIRE
Influencer	Uses interpersonal skills to non-coercively affect the actions and decisions of others	How do I know my influence – input has made the difference to the status quo? Write down some samples.	Look for opportunities to practice your interpersonal skills and different types of power. Start with small goals to increase your confidence
Change Agent	Raises difficult and challenging questions that others may perceive as a threat the status quo.	What are my motives for asking challenging questions? Does my question advance the cause or add roadblocks?	When initiating change, pick low in fruit first and build up your confidence as a change agent. Gain credibility and trust with those around you.
Future Minded	Having a forward-looking mentality and sense of direction and concern for where to be in the future. Able to see beyond your present contradictions.	What are others doing that is leading edge? Can I learn from them? What are the contradictions in my life?	Read widely from an international perspective. Dream of possibilities and potential developments, always keeping your eyes on the horizon. Develop an intentional international network.
Intentional Leadership	Is aware and proactive concerning strengths and weaknesses and has delineated goals for achieving personal best and influencing others.	What is my dominant leadership style/preference? Do I know my follower's needs? What do my short term and long term outcomes need to be?	When forming a leadership team make sure to select people who complement your weaknesses and are not afraid to talk to you about them.
Constructive use of Influence	Appropriately uses different types of power to create a desired image and influence.	Do I know how others perceive me? Am I aware of the actions that create those perceptions?	Consider critical feedback a gift and actively seek it out from others – especially those with whom you share values, but have different ideas.
Critical Thinker	Makes connections, integrates, and makes practical application of different actions, opinions, outcomes and information.	How aware am I of my thinking and reactions in real time? Do I self-edit in real time? Am I able to process, connect, and integrate information and practical applications?	Build relationships with colleagues that transcend the workplace. Ask for feedback to check out what was intended relative to what actually happened

(Continued from previous page)

BEHAVIOR	DESCRIPTION	KEY QUESTIONS	HOW TO ACQUIRE
Culturally Sensitive	Works to provide opportunities for diverse members to interact in a nondiscriminatory manner.	How inclusive am I of other's ideas? Do I believe that ideological differences equate to richness?	Look at who you interact with at work and in your community – be interested in their different experiences and background.
Multicultural Leader	Can influence the behaviors and attitudes of ethnically diverse people or groups	How well do I understand different cultures and worldviews?	Study world cultures and religions. When leading or forming teams, strive to include cultures and worldviews different from your own.
Communitarian	Expresses concern about social trends and issues and participates in civic and community activities.	Do I have a sense of social justice? Am I community minded? What do I do about injustice?	Become involved in a community or civic outreach. Ask friends and colleagues to join you.
Mission Minded	Communicates how the performance of others affects the mission. Is aware of how their own attitude affects people's perception of who they represent.	How familiar am I with the mission of my organization? Do I role model the mission and values I claim to promote outside of the organization?	Look for mentors in your organization who exhibit the values of the mission. Identify what makes them stand out. Practice their best qualities until they become second nature.
Consensus Builder	Convinces other people to see the common good or a different point of view.	What is it about the values and goals that will win the hearts and mind of others? What outcomes are attractive to others and why?	Practice painting the big picture in such a way that others are enthused, want to contribute, and participate.
Diagnoses Context	Knows how to appropriately interpret and react to shifts or changes in one's surroundings.	How aware am I of the contextual ethos? Am I resilient and adaptive to volatility in change?	Check out and evaluate your interpretation of the context with a colleague or friend.

Bibliography

1. Aarnoudse, A., Reeler, D., & Martin, T. (Eds.), (2011). The Barefoot Guide to learning practices and social change. South Africa: The Barefoot Collective.
2. Argyris, C. (1999). Tacit knowledge and management. In R.J. Sternberg & J.A. Horvath (Eds.), *Tacit Knowledge in Professional Practice* (pp. 123-140). Mahwah, NJ: Lawrence Erlbaum Associates.
3. Bamford-Wade, A.F. (2011). Surfing the Wave: leadership in turbulent times. *New Zealand Nursing Review*. May, pp. 16-17.
4. Benner, P. (2001). From novice to expert. Upper Saddle River, NJ: Prentice Hall.
5. Bettis, R.A., & Hitt, M.A. (1995). The New Competitive Landscape. *Strategic Management Journal*, *16* (Summer), 7-19.
6. Bird, B.J. (1992). The Operation of Intentions in Time: The Emergence of the New Venture. *Entrepreneurship: Theory and Practice*, 17(Fall), 11-20.
7. Blass, F.R. & Ferris, G.R (2007). Leader Reputation: The role of mentoring, political skill, contextual learning and adaptation. *Human Resource Management*. Vol.46. Iss 1. 5-19

8. Bluedorn, A.C. & Denhardt, R.B. (1988). Time and Organizations. *Journal of Management, 14*(2), 299-320.

9. Bluedorn, A.C., Kaufman, C.F., & Lane, P.M. (1992). How Many Things Do You like to Do at Once? An Introduction to Monochronic and Polychronic Time. *The Executive, 6*(4), 17-26.

10. Boisot, M. H. (1998). Knowledge Assets: Securing Competitive Advantage in the Information Economy. Oxford, U.K: Oxford University Press.

11. Bolden, R. & Gosling, J. (2006). Leadership Competencies: Time to change the tune? *Leadership,* 2 (2), 147-164

12. Brown, C. H., Gould, D. & Foster, S. (2005). A framework for developing contextual intelligence (CI). *The Sport Psychologist, 19*, 5–62.

13. Burns, J.S. (2002). Chaos theory and leadership studies: exploring uncharted seas. *Journal of Leadership and Organizational Studies, 9*(2), 42-57.

14. Calarco, A., & Gurvis, J. (2006). Flexible flyers: A leader's framework for developing adaptability. *Leadership in Action, 25*(6), 4-16.

15. Chan, A. (2000). Critically constituting organization. Amsterdam: John Benjamins

16. Das, T. K. (1986). The subjective side of strategy making; Future orientations and perceptions of executives. New York: Praeger.

17. Das, T. K. (1987). Strategic planning and individual temporal orientation. *Strategic Management Journal, 8*, 203-209.

18. Das, T. K. (1991). Time: The hidden dimension in strategic planning. *Long Range Planning, 24*(3), 49-57.

19. Das, T. K. (1993). Time in management and organizational studies. *Time & Society, 2*, 267-274.

20. Day, D. V. (2001) Leadership development: A review in context. *Leadership Quarterly, 11*(4), 581–613.

21. Dooley, K. (1996). A Nominal Definition of Complex Adaptive Systems. *The Chaos Network, 8*(1): 2-3.

22. Drucker, P. F. (1985). Innovation and Entrepreneurship. New York, NY: HarperBusiness.

23. Drucker, P.F. (2001). The Essential Drucker. New York, NY: HarperBusiness.

24. Endler, N.S., Magnusson, D. (1976). Toward an interactional psychology of personality. Psychological Bulletin, 83, 956-974.

25. Ericsson, K., Prietula, M. J., & Cokely, E. T. (2007). The Making of an Expert. (cover story). *Harvard Business Review, 85*(7/8), 114-121.

26. Feidler, F.E. (1967). A theory of effectiveness. New York: McGraw-Hill.

27. Ferris, G. R., Treadway, D. C., Kolodinsky, R. W., Hochwarter, W. A., Kacmar, C. J., Douglas, C., & Frink, D. D. (2005). Development and validation of the political skill inventory. *Journal of Management, 31*, 126–152.

28. Fleishman, E. A., Mumford, M. D., Zaccaro, S. J., Levin, K. Y., Korotkin, A. L., & Hein, M. B. (1991). Taxonomic efforts in the description of leader behavior: A synthesis and functional interpretation. *The Leadership Quarterly, 2*(4), 245-287.

29. Gardner, H. (1983). Frames of mind: The theory of multiple intelligences. New York: Basic Books.

30. Gharajedaghi, J. (2011). Systems Thinking: Managing Chaos and Complexity. Amsterdam: Elsevier.

31. Grant, R.M. (1996). Towards a Knowledge Based Theory of the Firm. *Strategic Management Journal.* Vol 17, Winter Issue, 109-122.

32. Grobman, G. M. (2005). COMPLEXITY THEORY: A NEW WAY TO LOOK AT ORGANIZATIONAL CHANGE. *Public Administration Quarterly, 29*(3/4), 351-384.

33. Hall. D. T. (2002). Careers in and out of organizations. Thousand Oak.s, CA: Sage.

34. Hays, K. F., & Brown, C. H. (2004). You're on!: Consulting for peak performance. Washington, DC: American Psychological Association.

35. Heifetz, R. A. (1994). Leadership Without Easy Answers. Cambridge, MA: Bellknap Press.

36. Jaques, E. (1982). *The form of time.* London: Heinemann.

37. Johansen, R. (2009). *Leaders Make the Future: Ten New leadership Skills for an Uncertain World.* Berrett-Koehler Publishers.

38. Jung, C. G. (1973). Synchronicity: An Acausal Connecting Principle. Princeton, NJ: Bollingen.

39. Knight, W. E., Moore, M. E., & Coperthwaite, C. C. (1997). Institutional research: Knowledge, skills, and perceptions of effectiveness. *Research in Higher Education, 38*(4), 419-433.

40. Kutz M. R. (2008). Leadership factors for athletic trainers. *Athl Ther Today.* 13:(4):15-20

41. Kutz M. R. (2010). Leadership and Management in Athletic Training: An Integrated Approach. Baltimore, MD: Lippincott, Williams & Wilkins.

42. Kutz M. R. (2010). Leadership in athletic training: implication for practice and education in allied health care. *J Allied Health.* 39: (4):265-279.

43. Kutz M. R. (2011). Contextual intelligence: overcoming hindrances to performing well in times of change. *Devel Learning in Org.* 25:(3):8-10

44. Kutz M. R. Toward a conceptual model of contextual intelligence: a transferable leadership construct. *Leadership Rev.* 2008;8:18-31

45. Lankua, M.J. & Scandura, T.A. (2002). An investigation of personal learning in mentoring relationships: content, antecedents, and consequences. *Academy of Management Journal, 45*(4), 779-90.

46. LePine, J. A., Colquitt, J. A., & Erez, A. (2000). Adaptability to changing task contexts: Effects of general cognitive ability, conscientiousness, and openness to experience. *Personnel Psychology, 53*, 563-593.

47. Lewin, A. Y. (1999). Application of Complexity Theory to Organization Science. *Organization Science, 10*(3), 215.

48. Logmen, M. (2008). Contextual intelligence and flexibility: understanding today's marketing environment. *Marketing Intelligence & Planning, 26*(5), 508-520.

49. Lorenz, E. *The Essence of Chaos.* Seattle, Washington: University of Washington Press, 1993.

50. Lusch, R.F., Liu, Y. & Chen, Y. (2010). The Phase Transition of Markets and Organizations: The New Intelligence and Entrepreneurial Frontier. *IEEE Intelligent Systems, 25*(1), 71-75.

51. Manville, B. & Ober,J. (2003, Jan). Beyond empowerment: Building a company of citizens, *Harvard Business Review*, 48–53.

52. Mayo, A. (2006, June). Contextual Intelligence in Leadership. Business World.

53. McGrath, J. E., Rotchford, N. L. (1983). Time and behavior in organizations. *Res. Organ. Behavior 5,* 57–101.

54. Mischel, W. (1977). The interaction of person and situation. In D. Magnusson & D. Endler (Eds), Personality at the crossroads: Current issues in interactional psychology. Hillsdale, NJ: Lawrence Erlbaum Associates, pp.333-352.

55. Osborn,R., Hunt, J. G., & Jauch, L. R. (2002), Toward a contextual theory of leadership, *The Leadership Quarterly 13,* 797–837.

56. Paul, R. W., (1995). Critical Thinking: How to prepare students for a rapidly changing world.

57. Polanyi, M. (1976). Tacit Knowledge. In M. Marx & F. Goodson (Eds.), *Theories in contemporary psychology* (330-344). New York: Macmillan,

58. Pulakos, E. D., Schmitt, N., Dorsey, D. W., Arad, S., Hedge, J. W., & Borman, W. C. (2002). Predicting adaptive performance: Further tests of a model of adaptability. *Human Performance, 125,* 299–323.

59. Rousseau, D. M. (1997). Organizational Behavior in the New Organizational Era. Annual Reviews, Palo Alto, CA, 515-546. Santa Rosa, CA: Foundation for Critical Thinking.

60. Schneider, M. & Somers, M. (2006). Organisations as complex adaptive systems: Implications of Complexity Theory for Leadership Research. *The Leadership Quarterly, 17*(4).351-365.

61. Schyns, B., & Schilling, J. (2011). Implicit leadership theories: Think leader, think effective? *Journal of Management Inquiry, 20,* 141–150.

62. Scouba, W. (2011). The Language of Discovery. *Journal of Biomedical Discovery and Collaboration, 6,* 53-69.

63. Senge, P. (1990). *The Fifth Discipline*: The Art and Practice of the Learning Organization. New York: Doubleday.

64. Senge, P., Scharmer, C.O., Jaworski, J., Flowers, B.S. (2005). *Presence: Exploring Profound Change in People, Organizations and Society*. Nicholas Brealey, London.

65. Smart, J. C. (2005). Attributes of exemplary research manuscripts employing quantitative analyses. *Research in Higher Education, 46*(4), 461-477.

66. Stacey, R. D. (1996). *Complexity and Creativity in Organisations.* Berret-Koehler Publishers.

67. Sternberg, R. (1988). *The Triarchic Mind: A New Theory of Human Intelligence.* New York, NY: Viking.

68. Sternberg, R. J., & Detterman, D. K. *(Eds.).* (1986). *What is intelligence? Contemporary viewpoints on its nature and definition.* Norwood, NJ: Ablex.

69. Sternberg, R., Wagner, R., Williams, W. & Horvath, J. (1995). Testing Common Sense. *American Psychologist,* 50 (11), 921-927

70. Terenzini, P. T. (1993). On the nature of institutional research and the knowledge and skills it requires. *Research in Higher Education, 34*(1): 1–10.

71. Tetenbaum, T. & Laurence, H. (2011). Leading in the Chaos of the 21st century. *Journal of Leadership Studies, 4*(4), 41-44.

72. Thoms, P. & Greenberger, D. B. (1995). The Relationship between Leadership and Time Orientation. *Journal of Management Inquiry, 4*: 272–92.

73. Uhl-Bien, M. Marion, R. & McKelvey, B. (2007). Complex Leadership: Shifting leadership from the industrial age to the knowledge era. *The Leadership Quarterly, 18* (4): 298-318.

74. Vaill, P. B., (1996*). Learning as a Way of Being.* San Francisco, CA, Jossey-Blass.

75. Vincent, K. (2007) Uncertainty in adaptive capacity and the importance of scale. *Global Environmental Change, 17*(1), 12–24.

76. Wagner, R. K. (1987). Tacit knowledge in everyday intelligent behavior. *Journal of Personality and Social Psychology, 52*, 1236-1247.

77. Wheatley, M. J. (1999). Leadership and the New Science. San Francisco: Berrett-Koehler.

78. Wheatley, M. J. (2006). Leadership and the new science (3rd Ed.). San Francisco: Berrett-Koehler.

79. Wheeler, J. (1957). On the nature of quantum geometrodynamics. *Annals of Physics, 2*(6), 604-614

80. Wilson, R. T. (1998). Servant leadership. *Physician Executive, 24*(5).

81. Winston, B.E. & Patterson, K. (2006). An Integrative Definition of Leadership. *International Journal of Leadership Studies. 1*(2),6-66.

82. Zaccaro, S., & Banks, D. (2004). Leader visioning and adaptability: Bridging the gap between research and practice on developing the ability to manage change. *Human Resource Management, 43,* 367–380.

83. Hastsopoulos, N. G. and Hastsopoulos, G. N. (1999) 'The Role of Tacit Knowledge in Management', in R. J. Sternberg and J. A. Horvath (eds) Tacit Knowledge in Professional Practice: Researcher and Practitioner Perspectives, pp. 141–52. Mahwah, NJ: Lawrence Erlbaum Associates.

THE RESEARCH BASIS OF CONTEXTUAL

INTELLIGENCE

The concept of Contextual Intelligence was formulated during the data analysis portion of an unrelated empirical investigation involving an exploratory factor analysis (EFA) of 49 leadership competencies. The EFA extracted 12 related leadership competencies from this larger list. During the creative process of examining and analyzing those 12 leadership competencies in light of their unique relationship to each other the notion of Contextual Intelligence was born. While Contextual Intelligence was validated as a leadership construct for that particular study, it is now expanded upon and introduced as a larger leadership construct.

METHODOLOGY

A two-phase research design investigating leadership behaviors of allied health care professionals was conducted. Phase One consisted of a mixed-methods Delphi Technique where 18 allied healthcare experts were asked to confirm or disconfirm as well as add to a list of leadership competencies identified in an extensive literature review. After two rounds of the first phase, the experts validated a list of 39 leadership competencies and added 10 additional leadership competencies resulting in 49 important leadership competencies for practice. This list of 49 leadership competencies was estimated to have acceptable internal consistency-reliability (Cronbach $\alpha = .96$) and interrater reliability (88%). Use of experts and a literature review established content validity.

The second phase was a national survey consisting of a blinded random sample of 161 allied healthcare workers ($\sim$10% response rate). 95% of respondents confirmed all of the 49 leadership competencies as important for practice. Scale reliability was estimated with a Cronbach $\alpha = .96$. Phase Two also consisted of an Exploratory Factor Analysis (EFA). Using a maximum likelihood extraction technique and promax rotation four leadership constructs were extracted. One of the factors extracted consisted of 12 interrelated meta-competencies ($\alpha = .90$) and was later named *Contextual Intelligence*. Construct validity was established by the EFA, convergent validity was established by Pearson r correlations ranging from $r = .43$ to $.94$ ($p=.001$) between the items within the factors, and concurrent validity was established through significant differences ($p=.05$) in independent t-tests and ANOVAs with post hoc adjustments between the four factors.

Three other leadership constructs were identified during the EFA. One was "Initiative," ($\alpha=.92$) which consisted of 14 metacompetencies and included demonstrating resilience, willingness to take risks, and responsibility. The third leadership construct identified was named "Communication and People Skills" ($\alpha=.88$) and consisted of 12 metacompetencies, and included demonstrating appropriate use of body-language, excellent verbal and written communication skills, and organizational savvy. The fourth leadership construct was delineated as "Personality Characteristics" (α=.93) and consisted of 11 meta-competencies, which include demonstrating assertiveness, ambition, and emotional stability.

Of the four constructs extracted, Contextual Intelligence had the highest mean rating (M=2.23, scale 0-3). This indicated that Contextual Intelligence was perceived to be the most important of the leadership constructs. Reliability and validity of the meta-competencies (skill set) that formed the construct of *Contextual Intelligence* is well established. The descriptor "Contextual Intelligence" was selected by the researcher based on the relationship of the individual items extracted, a review of the literature, and the theoretical concept illustrated in the Contextual Intelligence triad. Table 2 is a list and description of the 12 metacompetencies making up the construct of Contextual Intelligence. The presence of many or all of these meta-competencies in an individual may also serve as a predictor of Contextual Intelligence.

A limitation is external validity and small sample size. While the skill set of Contextual Intelligence is an exciting and promising leadership construct the concept was built on an empirical investigation of leadership competencies validated and generalized to a specific healthcare discipline, which is a threat to external validity. However, most (79.6%) of the leadership competencies were derived from a literature review that consisted mostly of business and management literature. Therefore, validating these skill sets for a wider population is promising. Additional research and inquiry on Contextual Intelligence is certainly needed. Furthermore, there are presumably other skills (observed behaviors) associated with Contextual Intelligence that are more difficult to delineate given the sheer number of possible contexts and the sheer number of variables associated within any contextual ethos. Understanding Contextual Intelligence and the many contextual variables and behaviors will always be, to a certain extent, conceptual.

Acknowledgments

No body of work, regardless of length, is done in isolation. There are so many people I need to thank and acknowledge for their help, encouragement, and support over the many years that I have been contemplating and developing this contextual intelligence model.

The first person that I must thank is my best friend and wife, Angie. She has been my biggest fan and greatest support. Without her input, graciousness in letting me stay up late hours and miss family meals to complete it, and her valuable critiques I would not have been able to even put together a coherent thought. I love you!

To my mom and dad who supported me and encouraged me in every phase of my life – and who were never afraid to discipline me, I say thank you. That discipline was the best thing that you could have ever done for me and taught as much or more about contextual intelligence than any studying ever could. Without a doubt I owe you both the largest debt of gratitude. You both instructed and modeled for me the most necessary skills to be successful: humility, respect, and servant hood. But beyond that you instilled me, the greatest and most rewarding thing of all, a love and passion for Jesus Christ.

To Nathan and Jonathan you are the reason why leadership is even important to me. You are a big part of motivates me. I know you both will be great leaders, even as young boys you already are! You are both called the change the world for the better. I hope and trust that you learn these principles, hide them in your heart, use them to do well in everything you put your hand to, but above all place the pursuit of Jesus, before any other pursuit and you'll discover that the rest is just details.

To my dearest friends and fellow leaders, Randy Kutz, Jason King, Matt Patchett, Tim Darnell, and JC Alzamora many of my ideas I have shamelessly stolen from you, your brilliant teachings and our exhilarating dialogues. I cannot say thank you enough for your time, friendship, encouragement, thoughtful critiques, and support. You make my life richer!

To George Barrett, you have been a true sage to me. A wise leader and mentor who has never been afraid to tell me how it is. You have been a mentor and father figure, so much of any good thing I have I owe to you and your guidance.

To my professional mentors I say thank you. Dr. Joan Scialli, Dr. John Cipolla, Dr. Norman Benz, Dr. Jack Ransone, and Steve Risinger you all have been very instrumental in how I came to contextualize the contextual intelligence model. Your teachings, examples, support and encouragement especially during my formative years, have been inspiring.

To my professional colleagues you have challenged me, challenged my ideas, and asked me the hard questions, thank you. Dr. Brian Campbell, Dr. Bobby Hill, Dr. Gretchen Carroll, Debra Ball – you guys are the best. Each of you brings to life an element of contextual intelligence that I would not have seen except for your leadership.

To my editor, Laurel Marshfield, thank you for your tireless editing and creative and insightful ideas to help make this academic diatribe at least a little more readable.

To my friends and family at Foundation Stone Christian Church, thank you for letting me be myself and being such a wonderful encouragement and blessing to me and my family.

To my readers, I say thank you and God bless you! I hope these ideas encourage you to pursue the best of your leadership potential. Always remember of the words of St. Paul who told the Roman church, "If God has given you leadership ability, take the responsibility seriously."

About the Author

Matthew R. Kutz, Ph.D. is a Fulbright Scholar, award-winning professor, textbook author, management consultant, and leadership researcher. But the words and titles that describe him best and the ones he most cherishes are husband, dad, and friend. He is on the faculty at Bowling Green State University's College of Education and Human Performance, is a popular conference speaker, and conducts seminars and workshops on Contextual Intelligence and many other leadership-related topics. He works with Fortune 500 companies, schools, hospitals, churches, professional associations, and other large profit and non-profit organizations. Some of his clients include: Procter & Gamble, Airtel, Ltd., Marathon Petroleum Co., World Relief, and ProMedica Health Systems

Matt earned his Ph.D. in Global Leadership from Lynn University in Boca Raton, FL, M.S. and M.Ed. degrees from the University of Toledo, and his bachelor's degree from Anderson University. He is the author of the widely used text *Leadership and Management in Athletic Training: An Integrated Approach* (published by Lippincott, Williams, & Wilkins). His research on leadership and sports medicine has been published in dozens of journals. He also teaches leadership and organizational development as an adjunct professor for Regent University, Central Michigan University, Palm Beach Atlantic University, and Spring Arbor University.

He has served as head athletic trainer for USA Track & Field's Team USA in international competition in Seoul, South Korea and Balneário Camboriú, Brazil. He is a USA Track & Field Level II Coach Educator, and sports medicine consultant and educator to the Honduran and Rwandan Olympic Committees.

Matt is influenced heavily by his faith. He is the son of a pastor (in fact, he even served as a pastor for three years and still functions as an ordained minister). His personal philosophy on leadership comes from Paul's letter to the Romans, where he teaches, *"If God has given you leadership ability, take the responsibility seriously"* Romans 12:8 (NLT). Matt subscribes to the belief that leadership is a serious responsibility that needs to be pursued and developed with diligence. He lives in Perrysburg, Ohio with the love of his life and best friend, Angie and their two sons, Nathan and Jonathan.

Contextual Intelligence Profile™

The CIProfile™ is a multi-rater assessment that consists of 48 self-rated questions and 15 peer-rated questions (can be distributed to up to 5 peers) designed to conveniently evaluate your current level of Contextual Intelligence. You can complete the profile at:

www.ciprofile.com

The Contextual Intelligence Profile™ produces five graphs (see sample on next page) that help you conveniently determine your overall Contextual Intelligence, 3D Thinking capacity, and how each of the CI behaviors contribute to your 3D time orientations. These graphs are valuable resources in the development of your Contextual Intelligence learning plan. They provide valuable insight on where to begin and what to focus on to increase your Contextual Intelligence.

The Contextual Intelligence Profile™ (CIProfile.com) is a way to inventory the behaviors contextually intelligent people demonstrate; as well as assess how those behaviors converge into your 3D Thinking (hindsight, insight, and foresight).

SAMPLE GRAPHS FROM CIPROFILE.COM

RIGHT: Sample *CI Circumplex* reveals your overall level of contextual Intelligence by illustrating how each of the 12 CI Behaviors work together. For example, the more contextually intelligent the "rounder" the inner-circle.

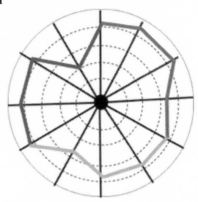

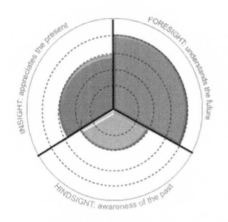

LEFT: Sample *3D Framework Circumplex* reveals the different levels of influence each of the 3D Thinking areas (Insight, Hindsight, and Foresight) have in how you relate to others and your organization.

BELOW: Graphs that illustrate how each of the 12 behaviors contributes to the individual time orientations. Provides valuable awareness of which areas are strengths and which need attention.

INSIGHT   HINDSIGHT   FORESIGHT

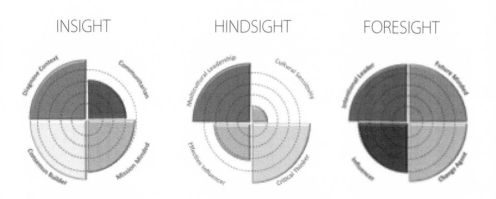

About Roundtable Group, LLC

Roundtable Group, LLC was founded in 2009 by Dr. Matthew Kutz to be a catalyst for leadership development and performance improvement. RTG provides exceptional development programs focused on leadership skills, executive-level thinking, and organizational performance. RTG strives to provide organizations with a high functioning and intelligent workforce. Based in Northwest Ohio RTG has a global reach, which offers learning-based solutions for global, regional, and local enterprises.

At RTG we are aware of the fierce competition you face. Your success depends on people who have the skill to handle those challenges. Let us help you create competent, high-performing, motivated employees so that your success can transcend socioeconomic boundaries. Through executive coaching, management consulting, or high intensity—high powered workshops we can help you position your organization for improvement and equip your people for maximum impact.
******

Roundtable Group, LLC is the exclusive provider of the *Contextual Intelligence Workshop*™ and publisher of the *Contextual Intelligence Profile*™.

Overview: Contextual Intelligence Model™

The world is experiencing an unprecedented pace of change. These dynamic conditions mean that leaders and top performers must intelligently navigate and adapt to constantly changing environments. This reality requires a new understanding of leadership, one that includes flexibility, adaptation, and resilience. The Contextual Intelligence Model™ delineates 12 specific behaviors that center around the need to embrace complexity, profit from synchronicity, and identify sources of tacit knowledge. The 12 behaviors are organized within a convenient 3D Thinking Framework™ (i.e., leveraging hindsight, insight, and foresight) and when demonstrated performance is able to keep pace with rapid and unexpected change. Developing Contextual Intelligence can help you diagnose your environment so that you can exercise influence in multiple contexts with a variety of different people and groups and helps adapt to uncertainty and ambiguity.

Overview: Contextual Intelligence Workshop™

The Contextual Intelligence Workshop™ is offered in one or two day formats. The content includes learning the 3D Thinking Framework™, participants are required to complete the Contextual Intelligence Profile™, which identifies their dominant three-dimensional thinking tendencies as well as identifies their level of execution on the 12 contextual intelligence behaviors.

Aspects of contextual intelligence discussed in the workshop:
- Non-Newtonian Thinking: Leveraging Complexity
- Synchronicity: Leveraging Experience
- Tacit Knowledge: Leveraging Intuition
- 3D Thinking: Leveraging Time Orientation
- 12 Behaviors of Contextually Intelligent People
- Actions Steps for overcoming obstacles and implementing CI

Contact Roundtable Group, LLC for pricing.
mkutz@roundtablegroup.net

Overview: 3D Thinking Framework™

Foresight is the proper relationship to the future. It includes the thoughtful anticipation of circumstances and events that have not yet occurred in order to inform present-day decisions. **Foresight helps put in perspective the positive and negative outcomes of the past.** It is an essential vantage point from which to relate to the past and present.

Hindsight is the proper relationship to the past. It includes the thoughtful and accurate memory of circumstances and events that have already occurred and cannot be undone. Hindsight is used in conjunction with foresight to inform present-day decisions. **Hindsight helps balance and put in perspective the anticipated future.** It is an essential vantage point from which to relate to the future and present.

Insight is the proper valuing of the present and requires the convergence of foresight and hindsight. Insight offers an acute awareness of the necessary actions for the present. **The present is the dimension where all decisions are made and life is lived.** Insight offers an essential vantage point from which to assess the value and necessity of past memories and experiences, as well as the usefulness of aspirational identity and goals.

Dr. Kutz's Workshop Topics

Workshops run 6-8 hours can be offered in one or two-day formats.

Contextual Intelligence Workshop™ [MOST POPULAR!]
Introduces the Contextual Intelligence Model™ and explains how to leverage Insight, Hindsight, and Foresight and integrate 12 behaviors of contextual intelligence. Includes session on how to interpret and apply the Contextual Intelligence Profile.

For the Greater Good: The Flow of Teams
Explains the power and nature of teamwork, how to form powerful and meaningful teams. Runs 6-8 hours can be offered in one or two-day formats.

Masterpiece Marriage Workshop (also features Angela Kutz)
Outlines the biblical roles of husbands and wife, includes in-depth session on identifying communication barriers and enhancing communication between couples. Workshop concludes with a detailed discussion on improving sexual intimacy between husband and wife.

Custom Workshops Available
Dr. Kutz can develop a customized training program to meet your specific educational needs.

Dr. Kutz's Presentation Topics

Note: this is not a full list. Presentations run from 60-90 minutes and can be offered as keynote and stand alone or breakout sessions.

Living a Non-Newtonian Reality
Explains how complexity and chaos can be used to gain momentum and creativity for contextually intelligent leaders. Includes a brief overview of Contextual Intelligence Model™

Tactical Efficiency: Demonstrating Strategic Intention
Delineates strategic intent from strategic planning. Outlines how developing strategic intent can reduce the frustration of uncertainty and volatility.

Leveraging Synchronicity
Learn how you can use experiences that appear to be unrelated and irrelevant to enhance your ability to influence others and contribute immediately in new or novel situations. Offers solutions for organizational "siloing."

Intentional Leadership: Getting People To Follow You
Explains how leadership can generate unwanted outcomes; and what you can do to help facilitate creativity and innovation in your organization or team.

The Significance Factor: Discovering Meaning in Volatility
Explains the phenomenon of "settling" for mediocrity, and teaches methods for improved passion and a proper work-life balance.

Leadership in a Nutshell
Introduces the basic concepts of leadership as distinct, but related to management. Asks and answers many common leadership questions and reviews common leadership theories, models, and research.

To complete the *Contextual Intelligence Profile*™
And determine your level of contextual intelligence go to:
www.ciprofile.com

To schedule Dr. Kutz for your even or a Contextual Intelligence
Workshop™ visit
www.roundtablegroup.net
mkutz@roundtablegroup.net